CMA
Part 2 - Financial Decision Making Exam

SECRETS

Study Guide
Your Key to Exam Success

CMA Test Review for the
Certified Management Accountant Exam

Dear Future Exam Success Story:

Congratulations on your purchase of our study guide. Our goal in writing our study guide was to cover the content on the test, as well as provide insight into typical test taking mistakes and how to overcome them.

Standardized tests are a key component of being successful, which only increases the importance of doing well in the high-pressure high-stakes environment of test day. How well you do on this test will have a significant impact on your future, and we have the research and practical advice to help you execute on test day.

The product you're reading now is designed to exploit weaknesses in the test itself, and help you avoid the most common errors test takers frequently make.

How to use this study guide

We don't want to waste your time. Our study guide is fast-paced and fluff-free. We suggest going through it a number of times, as repetition is an important part of learning new information and concepts.

First, read through the study guide completely to get a feel for the content and organization. Read the general success strategies first, and then proceed to the content sections. Each tip has been carefully selected for its effectiveness.

Second, read through the study guide again, and take notes in the margins and highlight those sections where you may have a particular weakness.

Finally, bring the manual with you on test day and study it before the exam begins.

Your success is our success

We would be delighted to hear about your success. Send us an email and tell us your story. Thanks for your business and we wish you continued success.

Sincerely,

Mometrix Test Preparation Team

Need more help? Check out our flashcards at: http://MometrixFlashcards.com/CMA

TABLE OF CONTENTS

Top 20 Test Taking Tips 1
Financial Statement Analysis 2
Corporate Finance 28
Decision Analysis 69
Risk Management 81
Investment Decisions 85
Professional Ethics 98
Practice Test 103
    Practice Questions 103
    Answers and Explanations 110
Secret Key #1 - Time is Your Greatest Enemy 121
    Pace Yourself 121
Secret Key #2 - Guessing is not Guesswork 121
    Monkeys Take the Test 121
    $5 Challenge 122
Secret Key #3 - Practice Smarter, Not Harder 123
    Success Strategy 123
Secret Key #4 - Prepare, Don't Procrastinate 123
Secret Key #5 - Test Yourself 124
General Strategies 124
Special Report: How to Overcome Test Anxiety 130
    Lack of Preparation 130
    Physical Signals 131
    Nervousness 131
    Study Steps 133
    Helpful Techniques 134
Additional Bonus Material 139

Top 20 Test Taking Tips

1. Carefully follow all the test registration procedures
2. Know the test directions, duration, topics, question types, how many questions
3. Setup a flexible study schedule at least 3-4 weeks before test day
4. Study during the time of day you are most alert, relaxed, and stress free
5. Maximize your learning style; visual learner use visual study aids, auditory learner use auditory study aids
6. Focus on your weakest knowledge base
7. Find a study partner to review with and help clarify questions
8. Practice, practice, practice
9. Get a good night's sleep; don't try to cram the night before the test
10. Eat a well balanced meal
11. Know the exact physical location of the testing site; drive the route to the site prior to test day
12. Bring a set of ear plugs; the testing center could be noisy
13. Wear comfortable, loose fitting, layered clothing to the testing center; prepare for it to be either cold or hot during the test
14. Bring at least 2 current forms of ID to the testing center
15. Arrive to the test early; be prepared to wait and be patient
16. Eliminate the obviously wrong answer choices, then guess the first remaining choice
17. Pace yourself; don't rush, but keep working and move on if you get stuck
18. Maintain a positive attitude even if the test is going poorly
19. Keep your first answer unless you are positive it is wrong
20. Check your work, don't make a careless mistake

Financial Statement Analysis

Common size and common base year financial statements

A common size financial statement is one that gives all figures as a percentage of a common base figure. This makes for easy comparison between companies. By formatting the financial statement this way it re4duces bias when analyzing two different size companies or when comparing the same company over various periods. A common base year financial statement is similar to a common size financial statement but it gives all figures as a percentage of an amount in the initial year.

Current liabilities

Current liabilities are those debts and obligations that are part of normal operations and that must be paid within one year. Examples of current liabilities are accounts payable, accrued expenses, short-term loans, that portion of long-term loans that are to be paid within one year. Current liabilities are normally paid using current assets.

Current assets

Current assets are those assets that can quickly, usually within one year, be converted into cash. Examples of current assets are cash on hand, cash held at a bank, accounts receivable, inventory, marketable securities, accrued income, and prepaid expenses. Current assets are used to finance the daily and ongoing operations of an organization and to pay expenses. Current assets along with current liabilities are used to calculate the current ratio and are used to determine an organization's liquidity and ability to pay short-term liabilities.

Current ratio

The current ratio, which is also known as the cash ratio, is calculated by dividing current assets by current liabilities. It is used to determine an organization's ability to pay its short-term liabilities using its short-term assets. The higher the ratio, the better able the organization is of paying its short-term liabilities. If the ratio is less than 1, it may mean that the organization will be unable to pay its current obligations when they become due. The current ratio is also a measure of how quickly an organization can turn products into cash. This is an indication of the amount of time it takes an organization to collect on accounts receivable or how long it takes to turn inventory into saleable products.

Management discussion and analysis

The management discussion and analysis is an addition to the financial statements. The management discussion and analysis is compiled by an organization's management and details the results of the organization's previous year of operations, the financial position of the organization, the cash flow, the liquidity of the business, and the organization's capital resources. In addition, management may also detail the short-term future for the organization. Future information may include the organization's goals for the upcoming year, new business prospects, and other changes that the organization may be considering. Also contained in this section is information about the management and the management style of the organization. The information contained in the management discussion and analysis is useful to those individuals who may be analyzing the information in the financial statements. Caution must be taken when reviewing this information because it has not been verified by an independent accountant and has not been audited.

Accounts receivable turnover

Accounts receivable turnover is calculated by dividing credit sales by the average of the beginning of the year accounts receivable and the end of the year accounts receivable. Accounts receivable turnover measures the amount of risk involved in an organization's accounts receivable. A lower turnover rate means that the organization is holding accounts receivable too long and may be unable to collect these obligations from their customers.

Acid test ratio

The acid test ratio is calculated by adding cash, accounts receivable, and short-term investments and then dividing the sum by the current liabilities. It is a measure of how well an organization is able to pay its current liabilities. It is the most stringent test of liquidity. Assets such as inventory and prepaid expenses are not included in this ratio because these assets usually take time to convert into cash. When the acid test ratio is lower than the current ratio, it means that the organization has a large investment in inventory.

Days sales outstanding in receivables

Days sales outstanding in receivables are the average numbers of days it takes for an organization to collect its accounts receivable. It is calculated by dividing accounts receivable by total credit sales and multiplying the result by the number of days in the accounting period. It is an indication of how well an organization turns sales into cash. A high days sale outstanding in receivables number shows that an organization has weak sales or is ineffective at collecting monies owed to it.

Days payable outstanding

Days payable outstanding is a measure of how long it takes an organization to pay its accounts payable. It is calculated by dividing accounts payable by cost of sales and multiplying the result by the number of days in the accounting period.

Days sales of inventory

Days sales of inventory measures the amount of time it takes an organization to turn inventory into sales. It is calculated by dividing inventory by the cost of sales and multiplying the result by the number of days in the accounting period. It gives an indication of the amount of time it takes to turn raw materials into cash. The goal is to keep a low days sales of inventory level.

Inventory turnover

Inventory is computed by dividing sales by inventory. It is used to determine the number of times inventory has been replaced over a period of time. When the inventory turnover ratio is low, it means that sales are low and that the organization has a high or excess level of

- 3 -

inventory. When inventory levels are high, an organization has made a large investment which does not have a rate of return. High inventory levels also mean that an organization may be in trouble if the price of their products goes down.

Liquidity index

The liquidity index is a measure of the number of days it takes to turn current assets into cash. It is calculated by first multiplying each current asset by the number of days it takes to turn each individual current asset into cash. Then the sum of this figure is divided by total current assets.

Operating cycle

The operating cycle of an organization is the amount of time there is between the purchase of inventory items and the collection of sales revenue. It is calculated by adding the number of day's inventory is held to the number of days it takes to collect accounts receivable.

Solvency

Solvency is a measure of how well an organization can pay its long-term fixed expenses on schedule and attain future growth. When an organization is solvent, it is in a positive financial position. When an organization is insolvent, it is unable to pay its expenses, has difficulties maintaining operations, and may be headed toward bankruptcy. Solvency and profitability are not the same. An organization can be solvent even though it is not making a profit. This may be due to the sale of accounts receivable to pay debts.

Capital structure

Capital structure is the method an organization uses to finance its operations. Methods of financing can be either equity or debt. Equity financing includes the issuance of shares in a public stock offering of either common stock or preferred stock and the use of retained earnings. Debt financing includes the sale of bonds and notes. The capital structure defines how risky an organization is. The riskiness of an organization can be computed using the debt to equity ratio. The more debt an organization uses, the riskier the organization.

Financial leverage

Financial leverage is also known as gearing or trading on equity. Financial leverage is the percentage of long-term debt to equity capital. It is a measure of how an organization finances its capital. Financial leverage is calculated using the debt to equity ratio. A high level of financial leverage means that an organization has more long-term liabilities than it has shareholder equity. A high level of financial leverage makes the organization a speculative investment.

Operating leverage

Operating leverage is the proportion of fixed and variable costs incurred by an organization. Operating leverage is measured using the fixed costs to total costs ratio, the percentage change in operating income to the percentage change in sales volume ratio, and the net income to fixed charges ratio. When an organization has a high level of fixed costs and a low

- 4 -

level of variable costs, its operating leverage is high. When an organization has a low level of fixed costs and a high level of variable costs, its operating leverage is low. When operating leverage is high, there is an increase in forecasting risk. This is because a small error in forecasting sales results in large errors in cash flow projections. In this situation, the organization is dependent on each individual sale to cover fixed costs.

Total debt to total capital ratio

The total debt to total capital ratio measures the amount of an organization's debt as compared to its total capital. It is calculated by dividing total liabilities by the sum of total liabilities and total equity. This ratio is used to determine an organization's capital structure and its financial solvency. The total debt to total capital ratio is affected when an organization issuing shares of stock, buys back shares of stock, takes out more debt, or pays off its existing debt.

Financial leverage ratio

The financial leverage ratio is the measure of an organization's financial leverage. It is calculated by dividing total assets by total shareholder's equity. The result is the total assets financed for each dollar of shareholder equity. The financial leverage ratio is used to determine how an organization uses debt to finance the purchase of assets. The higher the financial leverage ratio, the more the organization uses debt to finance assets.

Debt to total assets ratio

The debt to total assets ratio is a measure of an organization's financial risk. It shows how much of an organization's assets have been financed with debt. The debt to total assets ratio is measured by adding short-term debt and long-term debt and then dividing the sum by total assets.

Total debt to equity capital ratio

The total debt to equity capital ratio measures the proportion of debt and equity used to finance assets. It is calculated by dividing total liabilities by shareholders' equity. Shareholders' equity is equal to total assets minus total liabilities. The total debt to equity capital ratio is a measure of an organization's financial leverage. A high total debt to equity capital ratio means that an organization has financed its growth with debt financing. This can result in higher earnings because of the high level of financing. This is only true if the increase in earnings is higher than the interest cost of the debt.

Asset coverage

Asset coverage is an indication of how well an organization's net assets cover its debt obligations. Asset coverage is calculated by first taking the book value of all assets and subtracting intangible assets, current liabilities, and short-term debt. Then divide the sum by the total outstanding debt. Asset coverage is used to determine the extent of potential losses if the organization were liquidated. The disadvantage of this measure is that assets may not be liquidated at book value.

Common-size statements

A common-size statement is a type of financial statement. On the balance sheet, it shows each balance sheet item as a percentage of total assets. On the profit and loss statement, it shows each item as a percentage of revenue. This type of financial statement makes it easy to compare different time periods for an organization or to compare different organizations. When comparing two or more organization of different sizes, the common-size statement provides a uniform basis (the percentage figure) from which to make the comparison. When comparing two or more time periods for an organization, the common-size statement shows how the financial position of the organization has changed over time.

Earnings to fixed charges ratio

The earnings to fixed charges ratio is also known as the fixed-charge coverage ratio. It is a measure of an organization's ability to pay its fixed financing expenses out of profits. Fixed financing expenses include interest payments and lease obligations. It is calculated by dividing the sum of EBIT plus the fixed charge by the sum of the fixed charge plus interest. EBIT is earnings before interest and taxes. A high ratio means that an organization is in good position to refinance its debt obligations when those obligations become due.

Fixed assets to equity capital ratio

The fixed assets to equity capital ratio are a measure of an organization's ability to pay its long-term debt. It is computed by dividing fixed assets by equity capital. A fixed asset to equity capital ratio that is greater than 1 indicates that there is fixed assets that are financed using debt instruments.

ROI

Return on invested capital (ROI) is the money earned from an investment. It is a measure of profitability. Return on invested capital is calculated by subtracting the cost of the investment from the gain on the investment and dividing the sum by the cost of the investment. When the return on invested capital is a negative number, then the investment should not be considered. Different calculations for the same investment may have different results because the ROI calculation can use different figures for returns and costs. Because of this, the calculation can be used to suit different purposes. For example, marketers and financial analysts have different purposes when computing ROI. The marketer may use the revenue generated by the product and the expenses used to produce the product to compute ROI. The financial analyst may use the net income produced by the product and the value of the resources used to produce the product to compute ROI. ROI is normally used to measure the earning potential of an asset or product. It can also be used to measure an organization's profitability from operations which is a measure of the effectiveness of the organization's management. ROI is also a measure of how well an organization has met its goals, how its compares with its competition, or how it stands within its industry. In addition, financial professionals use ROI to determine how well an organization utilizes its resources and to determine its financial strength.

Times interest earned ratio

The times interest earned ratio is a measure of an organization's ability to pay its debt obligations. It is calculated by dividing the earnings before interest and taxes by the total interest payable. It shows how many times an organization can cover its interest payments on a pretax basis. A low ratio means that an organization may not be able to pay its debt obligations. A high ratio means that an organization either has very little debt or is paying off too much of its debt. A high ratio is undesirable because too much money is going into debt service instead of investing in new projects that could be used to increase the organization's income.

Return on common equity ratio

The return on common equity ratio is a measure of an organization's profitability. It is calculated by dividing net income by shareholder's equity. The return on common equity ratio shows how much profit the organization earns using the money invested in the organization by common shareholders. This ratio gives shareholders an indication of how well an organization is using the money it received from shareholder investment. It is used to compare different accounting periods for an organization and to compare one organization with other organizations within its industry. The return on common equity ratio does not adequately compare organizations that are in different industries.

Return on total assets ratio

The return on total assets ratio is a measure on how efficiently an organization uses its assets. It is calculated by dividing income before interest and taxes by current assets plus current assets. The result shows how much income is earned from each dollar invested in assets. A low return on total assets ratio means that the organization does not carry many assets. A high return on total assets ratio means that the organization has a high level of assets. Service and professional firms, such as accountants and software developers, normally have a small number of assets. Manufacturing firms are highly asset intensive.

Profit margin on sales

Profit margin on sales is used to determine an organization's operational efficiency. It is calculated by dividing net income before interest and taxes by sales. It shows how much income is received for each dollar of sales. An organization should compare its profit margin on sales over a period of time to reveal trends. When the profit margin on sales increases over time, it shows that an organization is becoming more efficient at using its resources. When profit margin on sales declines, the organization may be experiencing financial difficulties. Profit margin on sales can also be used to compare the organization with other organizations within the same industry.

DuPont model

The DuPont model is used to give a better understanding of return on equity. Return on equity is an important indicator of an organization's profitability and growth. The DuPont model shows the three components of return on equity to reveal where an organization receives this return. The DuPont formula calculates return on equity by first calculating its three components and then multiplying the three components. The three components are net margin, asset turnover, and financial leverage. Net margin is net income divided by sales. Asset turnover is sales divided by total assets. Financial leverage is total assets divided by average stockholder equity. By dividing return on equity into its components, changes in return on equity can be tracked over a period of time.

Equity multiplier

The equity multiplier is a measure of financial leverage. It is calculated by dividing total assets by total stockholders' equity. The equity multiplier is used to determine how an organization uses debt to finance assets. It measures the amount of assets per dollar of stockholders' equity. A high equity multiplier shows that an organization uses a large amount of debt to finance assets.

Total asset turnover

Total asset turnover is a measure of the amount of sales revenue received by an organization from each dollar invested in assets. It is calculated by dividing revenue by total assets. Total asset turnover indicates how efficiently an organization uses its assets to generate revenue. It also indicates an organization's pricing strategy. A high total asset turnover usually means that an organization has a low profit margin.

Dividend payout ratio

The dividend payout ratio is the percentage of earnings that are paid out to shareholders in the form of dividends. It is calculated by dividing yearly dividends per share by earnings per share. The dividend payout ratio gives an indication of the ability of an organization to pay out dividends. The longer an organization has been in business, the higher its dividend payout ratio is likely to be. Organizations that are in a growth stage will have a lower dividend payout ratio because earnings are usually reinvested in the organization and not paid out to shareholders.

Dividend yield

The dividend yield indicates how much of an organization's earnings are paid out in dividends each year in relation to the price of its stock. It is the return on investment for an organization's stock. The dividend yield is calculated by dividing the annual dividends per share by the price per share. It is a measure of the amount of cash flow that is received by a shareholder for each dollar invested in an organization's stock. For an investor who needs cash flow from their investments, a high dividend yield is needed.

Operating profit margin

Operating profit margin is also known as return on sales. The operating profit margin is used to determine an organization's operational efficiency. It is calculated by dividing net income before interest and taxes by sales. Operating profit margin measures the amount of profit is received for each sales dollar. It is used to look at trends over a period of time or to compare one organization with others in the same industry. When operating profit margin increases over time, the organization is becoming more efficient. A decreasing profit margin could mean future financial trouble for an organization.

Gross profit margin

Gross profit margin is the percent of sales dollars that are not spent on an organization's expenses. It is calculated by dividing gross income by net sales. A higher gross profit margin means that an organization has more money left over after it pays its expenses. This means that the organization keeps control over its costs. Gross profit margin is a better indication of an organization's earnings potential than looking at just earnings. Just because earnings increase does not mean that the profit margin increases. When an organization's costs have increased at a greater rate than earnings, the gross profit margin will go down.

Book value per share

Book value per share is the value of an organization's stock. This value is based on the historical cost of the stock. The book value per share of common stock is computed by first subtracting the liquidation value of preferred stock and the preferred dividends in arrears from the total stockholders' equity. Then, the sum is divided by the total number of common shares issued. The book value per share of preferred stock is computed by first adding the liquidation value of preferred stock and the preferred dividends in arrears. Than, the sum is divided by the total number of preferred shares.

Net profit margin

Net profit margin is a measure of the proportion of an organization's revenue that is retained after paying its variable production costs. Variable productions costs include wages and cost of goods sold. Net profit margin is calculated by dividing operating income by net sales. It is used to determine an organization's ability to pay fixed costs. Net profit margin shows how much income an organization makes before interest and taxes on each sales dollar. When looking at net profit margin over time, an increasing profit margin means that the organization is earning more money for each sales dollar.

DuPont Analysis

The DuPont Analysis is a form of decomposition whereby the expression for ROE (ROE = return/equity) is expanded into either three (profit margin, asset turnover, and equity multiplier) or five (previous three plus interest expense and tax retention rate) constituent variables. This allows the resulting measurement of ROE to be examined and understood in greater detail and provides for enhanced comparability among benchmark companies, prior period results, and planned results. The DuPont Analysis method consists of algebraically expanding and then resolving the basic two-variable equation (ROE = return/equity) in order to introduce the additional variables of sales and assets. In step one, each side of the equation is multiplied by the variable (sales/sales):

Step One—Sales Component (Multiply by Sales Divided by Sales) and Resolve:

1	ROE =	NET INCOME	/	SHAREHOLDER'S EQUITY

$$2 \quad ROE \times (SALES/SALES) = \frac{NET\ INCOME \times SALES}{SALES} \quad / \quad \frac{SHAREHOLDER'S\ EQUITY \times SALES}{SALES}$$

$$3 \quad ROE \times 1 = NET\ INCOME \times SALES \quad / \quad SHAREHOLDER'S\ EQUITY \times SALES$$

$$4 \quad ROE = \underset{Profit\ Margin}{NET\ INCOME\ /\ SALES} \quad X \quad \underset{Equity\ Turnover}{SALES\ /\ SHAREHOLDER'S\ EQUITY}$$

In step two (following step one), each side of the equation is multiplied by the variable (assets/assets):

Step Two—Assets Component (Multiply by Assets/Assets) and Resolve:

$$5 \quad \begin{array}{c} ROE \times \\ (ASSETS/ASSETS) = \end{array} \frac{(NET\ INCOME\ /\ SALES) \times ASSETS}{ASSETS} \quad X \quad \frac{(SALES\ /\ SHAREHOLDER'S\ EQUITY) \times ASSETS}{ASSETS}$$

$$6 \quad ROE \times 1 = (NET\ INCOME\ /\ SALES) \times ASSETS \quad X \quad (SALES\ /\ SHAREHOLDER'S\ EQUITY) \times ASSETS$$

$$7 \quad ROE = (NET\ INCOME\ /\ SALES) \quad X \quad (SALES\ /\ ASSETS) \quad X \quad (ASSETS\ /\ SHAREHOLDER'S\ EQUITY)$$

$$\textbf{Profit Margin} \quad x \quad \textbf{Asset Turnover} \quad x \quad \textbf{Equity Multiplier}$$

The above result is the final three-step equation for measuring ROE.

The three-step equation is expanded and resolved in a similar fashion as the original equation. Step one involves separating the tax value from net income (expressed as earnings before tax, or EBT):

$$8 \quad ROE = ((EBT \times (1 - TAX\ RATE)\ /\ SALES) \quad X \quad (SALES\ /\ ASSETS) \quad X \quad (ASSETS\ /\ SHAREHOLDER'S\ EQUITY)$$

$$9 \quad ROE = (EBT\ /\ SALES) \quad X \quad (SALES\ /\ ASSETS) \quad X \quad (ASSETS\ /\ SHAREHOLDER'S\ EQUITY) \times (1 - TAX\ RATE)$$

$$10 \quad ROE = \textbf{Profit Margin Before Tax} \quad x \quad \textbf{Asset Turnover} \quad x \quad \textbf{Equity Multiplier} \quad x \quad \textbf{Tax Retention Rate}$$

Step two (following step one) involves separating interest expense from net income (expressed as earnings before interest and tax, or EBIT):

$$11 \quad ROE = ((EBIT - INTEREST) \times (1 - TAX\ RATE))\ /\ SALES) \quad X \quad (SALES\ /\ ASSETS) \quad X \quad (ASSETS\ /\ SHAREHOLDER'S\ EQUITY)$$

$$12 \quad ROE = ((EBIT\ /\ SALES) \quad X \quad (SALES\ /\ ASSETS) - (INTEREST\ /\ ASSETS))$$

$$X \quad (ASSETS\ /\ SHAREHOLDER'S\ EQUITY) \times (1 - TAX\ RATE)$$

$$ROE = \textbf{(Operating Profit Margin} \ x \ \textbf{Asset Turnover - Interest Expense Rate)} \ x \ \textbf{Equity Multiplier} \ x \ \textbf{Tax Retention Rate}$$

The above result is the final five-step equation for measuring Return on Equity (ROE).

Example

Using the data provided, explain the change in the return on equity (ROE) between periods one and two using the standard equation (net income/equity).

	PERIOD 1	PERIOD 2
NET INCOME	$ 31,500	$ 42,000
EQUITY	$ 250,000	$ 283,600
ROE	12.6%	14.8%
INCREASE		2.2%

Using the standard two-variable equation, the ROE result can be explained in terms of two factors, net income and other changes to equity:

EQUITY

BEGINNING BALANCE	$	250,000
NET INCOME	$	42,000
OTHER ADDITIONS	$	(8,400)
ENDING BALANCE	$	283,600

If equity had been increased only by the amount of net income, the ROE would have been calculated as $42,000 / ($250,000 + $42,000) = 14.4%. Therefore, the additional increase in ROE of 0.4% is a function of the reduction in equity of $8,400 (presumably due to a stock buyback or dividend payment).

Using the data from the three-step DuPont Analysis provided, explain the change in return on equity (ROE) between periods one and two.

Unlike the use of the two-variable standard equation, which explains the increase based upon net income and equity only, the DuPont Analysis expands the explanation of change to include the effect of sales and assets:

- Net income (net profit margin) was favorably impacted by both an increase in margin rate as well as an increase in sales, both contributing to the higher ROE.
- Asset turnover was lower, indicating a disproportionate increase in assets relative to the increase in sales, unfavorably impacting the increase in ROE.
- Equity multiplier was higher, indicating that assets increased at a faster rate than equity, contributing to the higher ROE.

Accrual basis accounting

Cash basis accounting assumes that economic activity occurs only upon the exchange of cash. Accrual basis accounting broadens the definition of economic activity to include transactions that meet the criteria for recognition regardless of any exchange of cash. The criterion that is applied is specific to the natural accounting classification of the economic activity: revenue, expense, asset, liability, or equity. In all cases, the essential test for financial statement recognition is whether or not the economic event has been completed and the stated purpose has been achieved. For example, revenue is recognized only when realized and earned; expenses are recognized only when the benefits thereof have been consumed or lost. Whether or not an exchange of cash has occurred is irrelevant. Thus, the

- 11 -

measurement of income under the accrual basis appropriately matches revenues with related expenses, the result of which would be significantly different if dependent upon an exchange of cash.

Comparability of static measurements and dynamic measurements

Generally, static measurements are less informative than dynamic measurements. Comparability can be used to provide context with regard to profitability (i.e., using relative comparisons over time). Consider the following summary financial results:

SALES	$	400,000
COST OF GOODS SOLD	$	275,000
GROSS MARGIN	$	125,000
OPERATING EXPENSES	$	65,000
EARNINGS BEFORE INTEREST AND TAXES (EBIT)	$	60,000
INTEREST EXPENSE	$	15,000
EARNINGS BEFORE TAXES (EBT)	$	45,000
INCOME TAXES	$	13,500
NET INCOME	$	31,500
		8%

Upon examination, one could conclude that the results are favorable because the net result is positive (net income) and the 8% margin appears somewhat reasonable. However, consider the plan for the period:

SALES	$	550,000
COST OF GOODS SOLD	$	365,000
GROSS MARGIN	$	185,000
OPERATING EXPENSES	$	75,000
EARNINGS BEFORE INTEREST AND TAXES (EBIT)	$	110,000
INTEREST EXPENSE	$	10,000
EARNINGS BEFORE TAXES (EBT)	$	100,000
INCOME TAXES	$	30,000
NET INCOME	$	70,000
		13%

Given that expectations were far in excess of actual results, the previous favorable conclusion would be questionable. The point is that a measurement without comparability is far less useful and actionable.

Comparative analysis using profitability ratios and common size income statements

Profitability ratios provide a common, size-neutral basis upon which to compare financial results to plans, prior periods, benchmarks, peers and competitors. Ratios transform absolute numbers into relative terms that enable meaningful comparisons. Profitability ratios include the following:
- Gross margin: (sales – cost of goods sold) / sales
- Operating margin: operating income / sales
- Net or profitability margin: net income / sales
- Return on assets: net income / total assets
- Return on equity: net income / total equity

A common size income statement is an extension of profitability ratios whereby each line item is expressed in relation to a common basis, usually sales. The result is a series of ratios with which comparisons can be made.

Measuring income at detailed levels

While the overall financial results of a company certainly have meaning and can be used for comparability, determining the root cause of exceptions upon which corrective action can be taken is vital. Companies of significant size require an accounting system that supports income measurement (and key balance sheet items) at the organizational level where the operational activity occurs. Profit centers and cost centers need to be vertically established at subsidiary, division, or department levels and horizontally based upon market, geographic, or product segments. The overriding objective is to measure and rationalize the results of operating activity, determine performance against expectations, and identify key performance indicators (KPIs) and other drivers that explain the results. This detailed level information is then aggregated to create analytical and actionable information with which management can determine future direction.

ABC

Activity-based costing (ABC) is, as the name implies, a costing methodology whereby operational activity is used as the basis for assignment of indirect costs rather than traditional, more-simplistic allocation routines. The result is a more detailed and accurate measurement of the costs of operation. For example, a traditional method of applying utility costs to an operating unit might consist of a simple ratio, such as the percentage of employees, floor space, or products produced. An ABC method would seek to measure the activity of each discreet unit as well as the actual consumption of utilities and assign the costs accordingly. The key factors affecting the efficacy of an ABC system include the following:
- The ability to identify the key drivers of activities.
- The ability to relate the key drivers to products and services as well as business partners, such as customers and vendors.
- The availability of data and software with which to measure both activities and costs.

Revenue realization and revenue recognition

The method by which a company records revenue for financial reporting (and subsequent analysis by analysts and investors) varies based upon the type of business being performed. In general, the matching principle of generally accepted accounting principles (GAAP) requires that revenue be recognized only when realized and earned. Realization occurs when consideration has been received or is receivable with a high probability of collection. To be earned is to have completed the process of providing the goods or services. Once both criteria have been satisfied, revenue can be recognized (i.e., recorded in the general ledger and disclosed in financial statements). The degree to which judgment or other subjective determination can be applied can significantly affect the measurement of income. Such potential for earnings manipulation is a key consideration in the evaluation of the financial results of a company.

Revenue recognition methodologies
Multiple methods of revenue recognition exist to reflect the economic reality of specific industries. These methods include the following:
- Sales—Recognition occurs at the time of transfer of ownership (i.e., shipment or delivery).
- Percentage of Completion—Recognition occurs incrementally based upon completion of milestones, assuming the activity is contractually obligated and reasonably estimable.
- Estimated Total Cost—Recognition occurs incrementally based upon proportion of total costs incurred.
- Cost Recovery—Recognition is delayed until all costs have been incurred (the most conservative method).
- Installment—Recognition occurs based upon periodic billings that include a high probability of collection.

The degree to which judgment or other subjective determination can be applied can significantly affect the measurement of income. Such potential earnings manipulation is a key consideration in the evaluation of the financial results of a company.

Components of revenue and analysis of overall revenue results

The primary component of revenues is, naturally, the realized and earned benefit from the economic activities performed on behalf of a customer. If the revenue recognition method is based upon the shipment of a product and concurrent transfer of ownership, then the principal revenue item can be called *gross sales*. Other methods may employ different terminology, such as *billings* or simply *revenue*. However, the selling process may involve substantial other activity (often involving contra or offsetting items) ancillary to the actual shipment. Such activity is separately recorded in order to facilitate analysis and understanding and includes items such as the following:
- Estimated Returns
- Promotional Allowances
- Rebates and Discounts
- Markups and Markdowns
- Delivery Margin
- Other Fees and Services

Net sales (or revenues or billings) would thus be calculated beginning with the gross amount and adjusted for each of the ancillary items.

Example

Using the provided revenue information, identify and calculate the effect of the various components of revenue on the overall revenue totals.

Analysis and understanding is best facilitated by classifying the components in a manner that reflects the nature of the business, such as the following:

GROSS SALES	$ 610,000	109.9%
Less: Adjustments to quantity:		
ESTIMATED RETURNS	$ (28,975)	-5.2%
ADJUSTED GROSS SALES	$ 581,025	104.7%
Less: Adjustments to price:		
PROMOTIONAL ALLOWANCES	$ (18,300)	-3.3%
REBATES AND DISCOUNTS	$ (12,200)	-2.2%
MARK-UPS & MARKDOWNS (NET)	$ 4,500	0.8%
NET SALES	$ 555,025	100.0%
Other Revenue:		
DELIVERY MARGIN	$ 3,050	0.5%
OTHER FEES AND SERVICES	$ 7,625	1.4%
TOTAL NET REVENUE	$ 565,700	101.9%

Relating each of the line items to net sales enhances comparability to references such as plan, prior period, benchmarks, and competitors.

Methodology used to value inventory or product costs on gross margin

Companies that carry a significant volume of inventory with multiple layers of costs (i.e., changing purchase prices over time) must determine an appropriate methodology with which to measure the cost of each item sold or consumed. While the method chosen is intended to reflect the actual sequence of inventory movement, the measurement of gross margin and, ultimately, net income can be significantly impacted. Examples of such costing methodologies include the following:

- Standard
- Moving Average
- Specific Identification
- First-In, First-Out (FIFO)
- Last-In, First-Out (LIFO)
- Next-In, First-Out (NIFO)

- 15 -

Example: Assume the selling price of a product is $31 and the inventory profile is as follows:

			PURCHASE PERIOD						NEXT PERIOD
1	2	3	4	5	6	7	8		
$ 20	$ 20	$ 22	$ 22	$ 21	$ 24	$ 24	$ 28	$ 181	$ 29

STANDARD COST:	$ 24	FIFO	$ 20
AVERAGE COST:	$ 23	LIFO	$ 28
SPECIFIC IDENT:	$ 24	NIFO	$ 29

The gross margin would vary from a low of $2 (using NIFO) to a high of $11 (FIFO).

Components included in cost of sales and analysis of overall revenue results

In addition to the cost assigned to the product being sold or consumed, the cost of goods sold category can include numerous ancillary items such as indicated on the following example:

COST OF GOODS SOLD	$ 465,000
COST OF ESTIMATED RETURNS	$ (22,088)
PURCHASE PRICE VARIANCE	$ (13,950)
RESERVE FOR MARKET PRICE DECLINES	$ 13,020
DUTY, CUSTOMS, BROKERAGE	$ 6,200
RESERVE FOR EXCESS/OBSOLETE	$ 5,813
RESERVE FOR MARKET PRICE DECLINES	$ 3,488
BREAKAGE/SHRINKAGE	$ 2,325
	$ 459,808

Example
Using the provided sales and cost of sales, identify and calculate the effect of the various components of gross margin on the overall results.

Analysis and understanding is best facilitated by classifying the components in a manner that reflects the nature of the business as well as the relationship to sales / revenue, such as the following:

GROSS COST OF GOODS SOLD	$ 465,000	101.1%
Less: Adjustments to quantity:		
ESTIMATED RETURNS	$ (22,088)	-4.8%
ADJUSTED GROSS COST OF GOODS SOLD	$ 442,913	96.3%
Less: Adjustments to cost:		
PURCHASE PRICE VARIANCE	$ (13,950)	-3.0%
RESERVE FOR MARKET PRICE DECLINES	$ 13,020	2.8%
DUTY, CUSTOMS, BROKERAGE	$ 6,200	1.3%
RESERVE FOR EXCESS/OBSOLETE	$ 5,813	1.3%
FREIGHT, INSURANCE, TAXES	$ 3,488	0.8%
BREAKAGE/SHRINKAGE	$ 2,325	0.5%
NET COST OF GOODS SOLD	$ 459,808	100.0%

Combined with similar levels of detail for sales, the gross and net margin results can be analyzed and compared using the constituent components.

PPV

Purchase price variance (PPV) is an integral component of a standard costing methodology whereby the application of a cost to an item of inventory is based upon a standard. Where the actual purchase price of the item differs from the standard, a variance is created. Consider the following example:

PURCHASING ACTIVITY									NEXT
1	2	3	4	5	6	7	8		PERIOD
$ 20	$ 20	$ 22	$ 22	$ 21	$ 24	$ 24	$ 28	$ 181	$ 29

STANDARD COST: $ 22

COST OF GOODS SOLD BASED UPON STANDARD COST:	$ 176
COST OF GOODS SOLD BASED UPON ACTUAL PURCHASE COST:	$ 181
PURCHASE PRICE VARIANCE	$ 5

The company estimated the cost at $22 and set the standard accordingly. The actual purchasing activity yielded a cost ranging from $20 to $28. The resulting cumulative PPV of $5 represents additional costs to be recognized in the financial statements.

Product costs and period costs

Costs are categorized as product or product related when the ultimate disposition of the cost is inventory for sale. Product costs for a merchant consist of the wholesale price of the item purchased for resale plus the ancillary costs of carrying inventory (delivery, freight, brokerage, insurance, obsolescence, damage, etc.). Product costs for a manufacturer consist of all labor, materials, and overhead consumed in the manufacturing process. Period costs are those that are not applicable to the items to be manufactured or sold. They are often categorized as selling, general, and administrative (SG&A) expenses that are incurred in support of the actual operational processes. Examples include management, research and development, marketing, and financing. Product costs are most affected by accounting policy decisions as the method of costing itself represents a subjective determination by management of the relationship between costs and actual operational activity.

Categories of product and period
The major categories of product and period can be further delineated as follows:
- Product
  - Direct Labor
  - Direct Materials
  - Depreciation of Machinery and Equipment
  - Overhead
- Period
  - Selling Expenses
    - Sales and Marketing Labor
    - Advertising and Promotions
    - Incentives and Commissions
    - Bad Debts

- o General and Administrative Expenses
  - Management and Support Labor
  - Office Facilities and Supplies
  - Research and Development
  - Regulatory Compliance
  - Non-Income Taxes
- o Interest Expense
  - Debt Service
  - Discounts and Premiums
- o Income Tax Expense

Overhead

Expenses that are classified as overhead consist of period costs that are directly attributable, and thus assignable, to the products either manufactured or sold. Generally accepted accounting principles (GAAP) require that such overhead costs be classified as production or inventory costs, ultimately recognized in the financial statements as part of the cost of goods sold. Typical such overhead costs include the following:

- Rent
- Utilities
- Depreciation
- Insurance
- Indirect Salaries and Materials
- Training and Development
- Capitalizable Interest

Analysis of financial results for forecasting

Example
Using the example provided, explain how changes in operating profit over periods of time can be used to understand the variability of financial results and support forecasting techniques.

	PERIOD					
	1	2	3	4	5	6
SALES	$ 375,000	$ 412,500	$ 453,750	$ 499,125	$ 549,038	$ 603,941
COGS	$ 222,094	$ 238,373	$ 264,820	$ 298,477	$ 353,477	$ 352,475
GROSS MARGIN	$ 152,906	$ 174,127	$ 188,930	$ 200,648	$ 195,561	$ 251,466
OPERATING EXP	$ 67,500	$ 74,250	$ 77,138	$ 77,364	$ 52,356	$ 87,571
EBIT	$ 85,406	$ 99,877	$ 111,793	$ 123,284	$ 143,205	$ 163,895
INTEREST	$ 12,000	$ 12,000	$ 32,000	$ 10,000	$ 10,000	$ 2,000
EBT	$ 73,406	$ 87,877	$ 79,793	$ 113,284	$ 133,205	$ 161,895
TAX	$ 24,224	$ 28,999	$ 26,332	$ 37,384	$ 47,954	$ 58,282
NET INCOME	$ 49,182	$ 58,877	$ 53,461	$ 75,900	$ 85,251	$ 103,613
ASSETS	$ 578,614	$ 627,796	$ 681,159	$ 739,057	$ 801,877	$ 870,037
EQUITY	$ 401,614	$ 460,491	$ 513,952	$ 589,853	$ 675,104	$ 778,716

Examining a series of financial results over time, using common size measurements, such as profitability ratios, can provide insight in two different forms:

- 18 -

Identification of anomalies or exception items for further root cause analysis.
Determination of trends or patterns that can form the basis for forecasting models.

SALES	100%	100%	100%	100%	100%	100%
COGS	59%	58%	58%	60%	64%	58%
GROSS MARGIN	41%	42%	42%	40%	36%	42%
OPERATING EXP	18%	18%	17%	16%	10%	15%
EBIT	23%	24%	25%	25%	26%	27%
INTEREST	3%	3%	7%	2%	2%	0%
EBT	20%	21%	18%	23%	24%	27%
TAX	6%	7%	6%	7%	9%	10%
NET INCOME	13%	14%	12%	15%	16%	17%
ROA	8.5%	9.4%	7.8%	10.3%	10.6%	11.9%
ROE	12.2%	12.8%	10.4%	12.9%	12.6%	13.3%

Though the net income indicates a reasonable growth trend, further analysis would be required in cost of goods sold (periods 4 and 5), operating expenses (period 5) and taxes (periods 4–6). Adjusted for the anomalies, the ratios are useful for trend analysis.

Decomposition analysis

The decomposition of financial statements is the process of separating reported measurements into constituent parts. A classic example of decomposition is the use of the DuPont Analysis for measuring return on equity (ROE). In much the same fashion, other measurements can also be decomposed. Consider the following example using the return on assets (ROA) profitability ratio:

FINANCIALS			ROA BASE	ROA DECOMPOSED	
SALES	$	18,000	RETURN (NET INCOME)	(NET INCOME / SALES)	= Profit Margin
NET INCOME	$	450	divided by	multiplied by	
ASSETS	$	8,750	TOTAL ASSETS	(SALES / ASSETS)	= Asset Turnover
			$450	2.5%	
			divided by	multiplied by	
			$8,750	2.1	
			5.1%	5.1%	

The ROA was decomposed to introduce sales as a factor, resulting in the availability of three factors (net income, assets, and sales) to explain changes in the measurement over a time series.

Labor rate and labor efficiency variances

The labor rate and efficiency variances for both the actual versus standard and the actual versus plan are as follows:

	ACTUAL	STANDARD	PLANNED	STANDARD OVER/(UNDER)	PLAN OVER/(UNDER)
LABOR HOURS	27,542	28,840	28,525	(1,298)	(983)
LABOR EXPENSE	$ 342,500	$ 353,290	$ 349,431	$ (10,790)	$ (6,931)
LABOR RATE	$ 12.436	$ 12.250	$ 12.250	$ 0.1856	$ 0.1856
		LABOR RATE VARIANCE		$ 5,110	$ 5,110
		LABOR EFFICIENCY VARIANCE		$ (15,901)	$ (12,042)
				$ (10,790)	$ (6,931)

Labor Rate Formula: (Actual Rate – Standard/Planned Rate) × Actual Hours

Labor Efficiency Formula: (Actual Hours – Standard/Planned Hours) × Standard/Planned Rate

Multinational corporation

A multinational corporation is a corporation that has business operations, facilities, and other assets in a country other than its home country. These multinational corporations may have manufacturing facilities, warehouse facilities, agricultural operations, mining operations, transportation systems, communication systems, or sales offices in foreign countries to facilitate a global business structure. Their global operations are controlled through a central office in the office of their home country. The advantage of multinational corporations is that they create jobs, increase wealth, and improve technologies in developing and impoverished countries. The disadvantage of multinational corporations is that they may have undue influence over foreign governments, can exploit poorer countries, and may reduce job opportunities in their home country.

Financial challenges
Multinational corporations face many financial challenges. When a multinational corporation has shareholders' from a variety of nations, it must pay dividends in the currencies of those nations. Multinational corporations must deal with changes in currency valuations. Because of this there is a need to protect its working capital from the risk of devaluation from currency rates changes. The multinational corporation must look at the advantages and disadvantages between owning, leasing, and licensing. It must also determine how currency and government regulations affect each option. Currency rates also affect the multinational corporation's earnings because of changes in currency exchange rates. There is also an unknown factor that affects the future business operations of the multinational corporation. There is the risk that a foreign government may interfere with or terminate the operations of the multinational corporation.

Currency translation

Currency translation is the process of converting the balance sheet of a multinational corporation from one currency into another currency. This translation is performed using the current exchange rate. Currency translation is required by the Financial Accounting

Standards Board. The requirements state that assets, liabilities, and earnings of foreign subsidiaries be restated to a national reference currency. The foreign currency translation exposure that results is accounted for in an equity account in the balance sheet. The foreign currency translation exposure is the risk that the value of assets, liabilities, equity, or income will change as a result of the exchange rate conversion.

Functional currency and reporting currency

Functional currency is the legal tender of the nation in which a multinational corporation receives and pays most of its income and expenses. A multinational corporation that earns the majority of its income in the United States and pays most of its expenses in the United States uses the US dollar as the functional currency. Reporting currency is the currency that is used to disclose financial information in a multinational corporation's reports and financial statements. The annual and quarterly financial reports must disclose the currency in which the financials are reported. Reporting currency is of particular use when a multinational corporation issues American depositary receipts (ADRs) and reports earnings in a foreign currency. This is helpful because investors will need to perform the currency conversions.

Foreign currency transaction

A foreign currency transaction is a transaction that is paid in a currency other than the multinational corporation's functional currency. Foreign currency transactions occur when the multinational corporation buys or sells products and services on credit and the products and services are in a foreign currency. Foreign currency transactions also occur when the multinational corporation borrows or lends funds that are in a foreign currency. A gain or loss on this type of transaction may occur when the foreign currency is exchanged for the functional currency of the multinational corporation. The gain or loss is the result of changes in the exchange rate between the functional currency and the foreign currency between the date of the transaction and the date the currency was exchanged. These gains or losses are recorded on the income statement.

There are many methods that can be applied to insulate a multinational corporation from the risks of currency translation. One way to reduce the risk of translation exposure is the use of consolidation techniques for the multinational corporation's financial statements. Consolidated financial statements are financial statements that include the accounting records of the subsidiaries of the multinational corporation into the corporation's accounting records. This shows the multinational corporation and its subsidiaries as one group. Another method is to use effective cost accounting evaluation procedures. The foreign currency translation exposure is recorded in the financial statements as either an exchange rate gain or an exchange rate loss.

Net exports and net imports

Net exports are the value of a nation's total exports less the value of its total imports. The net exports number is used to determine a nation's aggregate expenditures. It measures the amount by which foreign spending on a nation's products and services exceeds the nation's spending on foreign products and services. The net exports figure is affected by prosperity of foreign nations, tariffs, and exchange rates. Net imports are when a nation's imports are greater than its exports.

Global trade

Global trade is a means by which nations trade with each other. Nations depend on trade to obtain resources in which they are deficient and to sell those resources that they have in abundance. A nation may lack the raw materials needed to produce the products and services needed by their citizens. A nation may have processed foods or finished products in excess of the needs of their citizens. A nation's available resources depend on its economy, capital, labor force, and land. Capital-intensive products, such as vehicles and machinery, are produced by industrial based nations. Labor-intensive products, such as clothing and consumer goods, are produced by nations that have low labor costs and modern production facilities. Land-intensive products, such as logging and farming, are produced by nations that have large quantities of usable land.

Comparative advantage

An economy has a comparative advantage over other economies when it can produce a product more efficiently and at a lower cost than the other economies. An economy can use this comparative advantage to import products at the lowest possible cost. By trading products in which the economy has a comparative advantage for products in which the economy does not have a comparative advantage, the economy can import products at a lower cost than the economy can produce the product. This method of exchange results is the most efficient use of resources for all economies involved.

Terms of trade

Terms of trade is the relationship between the prices at which a nation sells its exports and the prices paid for its imports. Terms of trade calculations do not indicate the amount of a nation's exports. It shows the relative changes between nations. A favorable term of trade is when the export prices are higher than the import prices. This is because the nation is receiving more imports for each unit exported. When a nation's terms of trade ratio go up, the nation is paying less for the products it imports. The nation is giving up less export for the imported products it receives.

Protectionism and barriers to free trade

Protectionism protects a nation's industries by imposing restrictions such as import duties, export bounties, domestic production subsidies, trade quotas, or import licenses. Nations that have large manufacturing interests support protectionism. During a recession, a nation may impose protectionist measures, such as a tariff, to protect its industries. A nation may impose protectionism to gain economic autonomy.

Advantages and disadvantages of free trade

Free trade is trade between nations without protective customs tariffs. Free trade fosters specialization, efficiency, and productivity. Free trade is mostly supported by economically powerful nations. When tariffs are low or non-existent, nations are willing to negotiate non-tariff measures to promote trade. These non-tariff measures include foreign direct investment, procurement, and trade facilitation. Agricultural nations favor free trade. It allows these nations to use their vast land resources to efficiently produce and export food, textile, and other crops. Free trade does not allow any room to protect a nation's industries that cannot compete effectively against foreign competition. Without protection, these industries may fail.

Import quotas

Import quotas are a type of trade barrier used by a nation to protect their businesses. An import quota limits the amount of a foreign product that can be imported into a nation.

Tariffs

A tariff is an excise tax that a nation imposes on imported products. Tariffs may be applied to an imported product that is produced within the nation. This generates revenue for the nation. This tariff is usually low and has little affect on trade. When a nation's manufacturers are at a disadvantage against imported products, a protective tariff may be applied to the imports. This increases the price of foreign products.

Export-Import Bank

The Export-Import Bank was created in 1934 as a federal agency to finance exports of U.S. products. It provides loans, credit guarantees, and insurance. The Export-Import Bank helps exporters obtain capital to purchase inventory or raw materials, market exports, or engage in manufacturing activities. Insurance is made available to protect against losses that may be incurred when dealing with the commercial and political risks of developing countries.

Effects of nontariff barriers

Nontariff barriers are used by nations to protect their businesses. A nontariff barrier imposes special regulations on foreign products that are imported into a nation. These barriers come in the form of requirements for licenses, permits, or other paperwork that make it difficult to import into the nation. This increases the price of the imported product, delays the delivery of the product, and can be frustrating. By imposing a nontariff barrier, a nation discourages foreign nations from entering their economy. The goal of this strategy is to limit the number of products imported to the nation.

Major international trade agreements

The first organization to foster world trade is the General Agreement on Tariffs and Trade (GATT) created in 1947. There are over one hundred countries that are signatories to GATT. The purpose of GATT is to foster equal treatment for all member nations, reduce tariffs, and eliminate import quotas. The European Economic Community (EEC) was formed in 1958. The purpose of the EEC is to create equal and fair tariffs for all of the EEC nations to promote trade in Europe. In 1989, the United States and Canada entered into the U.S. Canadian Free Trade Agreement in 1989. This agreement removed trade barriers between the two nations. In 1994, the United States, Canada, and Mexico signed the North American Free Trade Agreement (NAFTA). This agreement created a free-trade zone among the three nations.

Customs union, common market, and economic union

A customs union is an organization of nations that has agreed to eliminate customs restrictions between members and to impose a uniform tariff with non-members. A common market is an organization of nations that is formed to facilitate trade, lower regulatory requirements, and reduce trade barriers between members. An economic union is an organization of nations that has a common currency.

Real income

Real income is the amount of products and services that can be purchased today compared to the price of those same products and services at another time period. Real income calculates the effect of inflation on purchasing power. If wages increase by 5% over the year and inflation was 3% for the year, the increase in real income is only 2%. If it costs $3,000 more per year to pay household expenses and annual income only increases by $2,000 per year, real income has decreased by $1,000.

Inflation

Inflation occurs when there is an increase in consumer prices or a decrease in purchasing power. This state is caused when there is more money and credit available relative to the production of products and services. In other words, the supply of money is increasing more rapidly than the demand for money. Over the long-term, a dollar will buy a smaller amount of products and services. Under these conditions, consumers will spend more dollars on those products and services they purchase. More money spent on consumption means that there will be a lower rate of savings.

Demand-pull inflation
Demand-pull inflation exists when an increase in consumer demand causes an increase in inflation. When consumers purchase more of a product or service, there becomes less of the product or service available. The price of the product or service will increase to effect a decrease in demand. This increase in inflation occurs as gross domestic products goes up and unemployment goes down. Inflation is only a temporary condition. As prices go up, more suppliers will begin to produce products and services to meet the increased demand and prices will once again go down.

Effects on an economy
A period of inflation may be good for an economy. Inflationary and deflationary periods can create a chance for prices to adjust. This price adjustment can help stimulate business and increase wages so that purchasing power is maintained. A constant price level that does not fluctuate will produce reduced profits and unemployment. Not all investors profit from inflation. Stockholders will see gains from the increase in business profits. Bondholders lose purchasing power because of the fixed percentage paid by the bonds.

Off-balance sheet financing

Off-balance sheet financing occurs when an organization makes a large capital expenditure and that expenditure is not recorded in the financial records of the organization. This type of financing does not create a debt on the organization's balance sheet. The organization is able to keep this information off of the balance sheet by using various classification methods. Examples of off-balance sheet financing include joint ventures, research and development partnerships, operating leases, the sale of receivables with recourse, take-or-pay contracts, letters of credit, and bank guarantees. Operating leases are the most common form of off-balance sheet financing methods. This method is accomplished because the asset is the property of the lessor and the lessee only reports the rental expense for the use of the asset. Organizations use off-balance sheet financing to keep debt to equity and leverage ratios low. It is also used so that the borrowing capacity of the organization is not affected.

Cost-push inflation

Cost-push inflation occurs when prices go up because production costs go up. The costs production can go up from increased wages or higher prices for raw materials. When the cost of production goes up, prices generally go up. Prices may go up when the demand for raw materials is greater than the supply of raw materials. This results in fewer products being produced while there is a constant demand. Cost-push inflation is most prevalent when there are not any suitable alternative products or services available to consumers. When the product or service is an important commodity in an economy, an increase in the price will cause an increase in the price of other related products. For example, an increase in the price of oil will increase transportation costs and any product that is transported to its market.

Going concern

A going concern is an organization that does not foresee the possibility of going out of business in the near future. A going concern has the necessary cash and other resources to continue to operate profitably. An organization that is not a going concern is either in the process of liquidation, headed toward bankruptcy, or has gone bankrupt. If an organization's accountant or auditor feels that the organization cannot continue business operations during the 12 months following a financial statement period, the accountant or auditor is required to disclose this fact in the notes to the financial statements. When investors and creditors feel that an organization is no longer a going concern, they may perceive the organization as being too risky. They may choose to sell their stock ownership in the company or attempt to recover loans made to the organization.

Factors affecting organization's finanical statements

Deferred income taxes
Deferred income taxes are taxes that will be paid in the future on income that has been earned and recognized in the financial records but not yet received. This is an estimated amount of future taxes due. When deferred taxes are recorded in the financial records, they are recorded as a tax expense in the income statement and a tax payable in the balance sheet. If the estimated tax is greater than the actual tax paid, the tax paid is deducted from the cash account on the balance sheet and the difference between the estimated and actual amount is deducted from both the tax payable account and the tax expense account.

Discontinued operations
Discontinued operations are those areas of an organization's business that have been sold, abandoned, or disposed of. Discontinued operations are reported separately in an organization's financial statements. In addition, if an area of operation in an organization is planned to be sold or the sale is pending, it is also reported as discontinued operations even

if the organization still receives income or incurs expenses on behalf of the operation. These revenues and expenses are reported in the year in which they were incurred. These earnings and expenses are not accrued. To qualify as discontinued operations, the area to be sold must meet the following criteria: the operations and cash flow will no longer be a part of the ongoing operations of the organization and the organization will not be involved in the operation of the area.

Stock options
Stock options are a right given to the owner of shares of an organization's stock. The option gives the shareholder the right to purchase a specified number of shares of stock at a specified amount on a specified date. Stock options are normally granted to the management and employees of an organization as a bonus for services rendered. The organization will record the stock option during the period when the service was performed. The amount to be recorded is the market price (at the measurement date) of the stock less the amount the employee is to pay for the option. The measurement date is the date on which the organization grants the option and determines the option price. When the option is granted, the organization records the transaction as a compensation expense on the income statement and as deferred compensation in the shareholders' equity section of the balance sheet.

Change in accounting principles
A change in accounting principle occurs when an organization changes the method by which it records financial information. Examples of changes in accounting principles include switching from cash accounting to accrual accounting, changing a depreciation method, or changing inventory methods from LIFO to FIFO. This change is recorded in the financial statements in the year in which the change occurred. The financial account in which this change is recorded is called the cumulative effect of a change in accounting principle and is part of the income statement. This change also requires an explanation in the notes to the financial statement and the change must be justified. In addition, some changes, such as changes in inventory methods, require that prior year financial statements be reissued to reflect this change so that the current year financials and the previous years' financials will be easier to compare.

Extraordinary items
An extraordinary item is a gain or loss incurred by an organization that rarely happens and is an unusual part of the organization's business. In most cases, extraordinary items are unforeseen and are not a typical event experienced by the organization. These gains and losses are reported as separate items in the organization's financial statements and are recorded as one-time charges. Extraordinary items are shown separately on the income statement. They are reported after income from discontinued operations and before changes in accounting principles. Examples of extraordinary items include losses due to a casualty (such as a tornado or hurricane), seizure of property by a foreign government, gains or losses on early repayments of long-term debt, and the write-off of an intangible asset.

Accrual accounting

Accrual accounting is a method of recording transactions when they occur and not when cash is received or when the transaction is paid. This method gives a more accurate picture of an organization's financial situation because future cash inflows and outflows are recognized in the financial records. The disadvantage is that accrual accounting requires additional time and monetary investment to implement. It is also a more complex system of accounting than cash basis accounting. In cash basis accounting, transactions are not recorded until the cash has been received or paid. For example, organizations that use cash accounting methods do not carry accounts receivable or accounts payable on their financial records. This makes it difficult to determine what future cash flows will be for the organization. In accrual accounting, revenues and expenses are recognized at the time of the transaction. Also, the revenue is matched to the expense; for example the sale of a product is matched to the purchase of materials.

Corporate Finance

Rate of return

A rate of return is the gain or loss incurred by an investment and is a measure of profitability. It is the comparison of the investment's earnings or losses to the amount of money originally invested. In order to compute a rate of return, an investment must be purchased and must realize cash flow at a future date. The cash flow may be in the form of dividends received while the investment is held or capital gains realized when the investment is sold. The rate of return is also determined by the amount of time the investment was held or owned. Usually, the rate of return is adjusted so that the percentage is based on a one-year holding period, even though the investment may have been held for a longer or shorter period of time. If the investment is held for longer than a year, the effects of compounding interest are also taken into consideration. The time value of money is also considered due to changing monetary rates in the international market. Inflation is also a factor in that it reduces the value of the money invested.

Expected return, standard deviation of return, and coefficient of variation

Expected gain is a measure of the most likely outcome of a gain or loss on an investment weighted by the chance of the gain or loss occurring. Standard deviation of return looks at the annual rate of return on an investment in order to measure the investment's risk. The higher the standard deviation, the higher the risk. Coefficient of variation determines an investment's level of risk in relation to the financial markets.

Relationship between risk and return on investments

Risk and return determines the potential gains and losses on investments. A gain on an investment is the return whereas the risk is the possibility of losing some or all of the investment made. There is a corresponding relationship between risk and return. If an investment has a high risk, it most likely has a high return. If an investment has a low risk, the potential gain is also low. Well-established organizations that pay a regular dividend are considered to be low risk. They also provide a low cash flow or gain on the investment. Growth companies are considered high risk and the potential for gains can also be high.

Systematic risk and unsystematic risk

Systematic risk is a type of risk where the entire financial market is at risk. With systematic risk, the investor has no control over the market conditions and diversification may not help reduce losses. However, hedging techniques can be used to help reduce losses. Systematic risk occurs when there are changes in the interest rates, a recession, a stock market crash, or a war. Unsystematic risk only affects a small number of investments. Unsystematic risk may occur when a company is faced with a lawsuit or there is an industry shakeout. Unsystematic risk may be reduced or eliminated by maintaining a diversified portfolio.

Managing risk to maximize return on investment

To ensure that an investment is as low risk as possible, all potential risks need to be examined. Once these risks are known, a plan needs to be put into place so that risk can be handled in a way that it minimizes losses and takes full advantage in any gains that may be realized. Risk management is different for different investors. If an investor is looking to realize a large profit and is not concerned about safety of principal, a riskier stock such as a growth stock may be purchased. If safety of principal is key, an investor may invest in low risk investments such as government bonds.

Value at Risk

Value at Risk is a measurement used to determine how much an investment or a portfolio will decrease over a short period of time in normal investment market conditions. To measure Value at Risk, several factors need to be considered. The amount of time the investment will be held is usually between 1 and 10 days. The confidence level is the measure of whether or not the investment will incur losses above a certain amount given normal market conditions. These two factors determine the level of risk of the investment. For most Value at Risk calculations, historical data is used to determine future financial market trends.

Hedging

Hedging is a method used to reduce risk caused by the price fluctuations of commodities. When the price of a commodity goes down, an organization will lose money on any commodities it owns. This risk can be reduced by agreeing to sell the commodity at a certain price in the future. Hedging is used by farmers and other agricultural businesses. To reduce the risks involved in the wheat market, a farmer may agree to sell his wheat before he plants the wheat and will set a specified price. The farmer receives the money at the time of planting but does not have to deliver the wheat until harvest time. By hedging, the farmer is assured of a certain dollar amount for his commodity and does not have the worries of taking a loss in case the price of wheat goes lower than what he has invested in the planting and harvesting of the wheat.

Bonds

A bond is a method that corporations, governments, and municipalities use as a long-term financing vehicle. The organization that issues the bonds pays the purchaser of the bonds interest over the life of the bond. In addition, the bond issuer repays the bondholder the invested amount at the end of the bond term. Corporate bonds are sold at either par value (or face value), at a discount rate (below face value), or at a premium (above face value). When the bonds mature, the corporation pays the bonds back at par value. The price at which the bonds sell is determined by whether the stated (or coupon or nominal) interest rate is above or below the market interest rate. Governments sell bonds to borrow money to cover spending when there has not been enough tax dollars collected. The federal government sells T-bonds. State and local governments sell municipal bonds. Municipal bonds can be either general obligation or revenue bonds. General obligation bonds are repaid from tax dollars and are used to finance government obligations such as schools and roads. Revenue bonds are sold to finance income generating projects such as airports.

Stock

Stock is the ownership vehicle of a corporation. This ownership is represented by shares of stock which gives the owner a claim on the corporation's earnings and assets. Common stock gives the shareholder the right to vote at shareholder meetings. Preferred stock has a higher claim on assets than common stock and pays dividends, but does not include voting rights. Treasury stock is shares of stock that has been repurchased by the corporation. Treasury stock has no voting rights, does not pay dividends, and is not considered in the shares outstanding calculations.

Preferred stock
Preferred stock is a method of selling ownership in a corporation. Preferred stock pays a set dividend and this dividend is paid before any dividends are paid on common stock. Preferred shareholders have the security of a known cash flow from dividends and the capital appreciation of the stock's value in the market. Although, preferred stock does not gain the market value as realized by common stock. Preferred shareholders do not have any voting rights in the corporation.

Common stock
Common stock is a method of financing used by corporations. Investors of common stock are owners of the corporation and have voting rights. Common stock may also pay a dividend to the shareholder. But, these common stockholders are on the bottom of the priority list if the corporation is liquidated and the assets of the corporation distributed among its owners. Bondholders, preferred shareholders, and debtholders are paid before common stockholders. The advantage to investing in common stock is the potential for a greater return than investing in the same corporation's bonds and preferred stock.

Par value stock and no-par stock
Shares of stock in a corporation are issued at a variety of values. Par value stock is the value of a stock which is determined by the issuing corporation. In some cases, this par value is the price at which the stock was offered in the initial public offering of the corporation. In other cases, the par value is a minimum amount, such as one penny. No-par stocks do not have a par value printed on the stock certificate.

Stock options and warrants
A stock option is a right sold by one party to another party that gives the buyer the choice to buy or sell a stock at a specified price within a specified period of time. Stock options are usually only good for a period of one month. Stock options can be used as an employment compensation vehicle. It may be given to management or employees for specific services rendered. In most cases the option price for the stock is significantly lower than the market price of the stock. A warrant is a security that gives the owner of the warrant the right to purchase stock at a specified price. Warrants are usually good for a period of years. This price is normally higher than the market price at the time the warrant is issued. Warrants can be sold along with bonds and preferred stock. In these cases, warrants are used to help lower the interest rate. The warrants are separate from the bond and preferred stock and the owner can sell the warrant independently of the bond or preferred stock.

EMH
Essential principals and the random walk theory: The efficient market hypothesis (EMH) holds that, at any given point in time, all relevant information related to stocks trading in a

highly liquid market (i.e., an efficient market) is incorporated into the price of each stock. Whenever new information becomes available, investors (who are assumed rational) incorporate the information into their market expectations, and the pricing is adjusted accordingly; the market is always efficient. As a result, according to the hypothesis, there is no information available to an investor that can provide a trading advantage over other investors or in excess of the market average. EMH is consistent with another theory, that of the random walk, which holds that stock prices move in a random manner (in other words, a random walk) and that past performance cannot be used to accurately predict future performance. In fact, stock prices cannot be predicted at all because all price movement is random.

Weak, semi-strong, and strong forms: Under the weak form of EMH, stock prices are assumed to reflect all information that is currently available at any point in time. The weak form follows the random walk argument that past pricing (and volume) have no relationship to future performance (prices move randomly), thus rendering the practice of technical analysis (the use of statistics, graphs, and charts) ineffective. The semi-strong form of EMH builds upon the weak form, holding that stock prices not only reflect all past information but also adjust immediately to any new information not previously considered. As a result, the semi-strong form also renders the practice of fundamental analysis (the use of micro and macro industry and company analysis) ineffective. The strong form of EMH extends the semi-strong form to hold that stock prices instantly adjust to any hidden or insider information as well as that which is publicly available.

Effects on passive or active investment management strategies: Because EMH holds that stocks are priced to include all available information, either public or private, an active investment strategy (i.e., picking winners and losers in an attempt to achieve returns greater than average) would be useless as price movements are simply random. If EMH is true, then a passive strategy based upon an index model would be all that is necessary. Such a strategy would attempt to buy and hold a portfolio that mirrors the components of an index (such as the S&P 500) and achieve the same return as the market.

Dividends

Dividends are the distribution of a corporations earnings to its shareholders. The board of directors of a corporation elects whether or not to pay a dividend to shareholders. Some corporations pay a dividend on a regular basis, some pay dividends only when they do not need the profits to expand the business, and some rarely if ever pay a dividend. Shareholders in corporations that pay regular dividends are looking for a consistent cash flow. Shareholders in corporations that rarely pay dividends are looking for growth in the price of the corporation's stock. When the board of directors of a corporation votes to distribute a dividend, this is the declaration date. On this date, the form and amount of the dividend is decided and the date on which the dividend is to be paid is also decided. Then, a record date is selected. This is the date on which the list of shareholders is compiled. Only shareholders on record on this date will receive a dividend. Finally, a payment date is selected. This is the date on which the dividend is sent to the shareholders of record.

Dividends paid on preferred stock are usually paid at a specified annual rate. Dividends on preferred stock are paid before dividends on common stock. Dividends paid on common stock may vary with the earnings of the corporation. After preferred dividends are paid, the remainder of the earnings will be distributed to common shareholders. In years with low earnings, the common shareholders may not receive any dividends. Preferred stock dividends may be cumulative or noncumulative. For cumulative dividends, any dividend not paid from current earnings will need to be paid in the next or future years along with the dividends for those years.

Types
A dividend is a distribution of a corporation's earnings to its shareholders. The dividend may take the form of cash, stock, or property. The declaration of a dividend is decided upon by the board of directors who also determine which class of shareholders will receive the dividend. A dividend is usually quoted in a dollar amount per share to be distributed. Cash dividends are the most popular type of dividend. Cash dividends are paid when a corporation has earned income and have excess cash on hand. Dividends paid in the form of notes are called script dividends. Script dividends are rare. Script dividends are paid by a corporation that has earnings that are expected to be turned into cash before the notes are due.

Stock dividends occur when a corporation issues additional shares of the corporation's own stock. In a stock dividend, a shareholder's percentage of ownership does not increase or decrease. The stock dividend is distributed on a pro rata basis. Stock splits occur when old shares are replaced with a larger number of new shares. Stock splits reduce the market price per share of the corporation's stock. Liquidation dividends are the return of capital in a corporation that is being terminated. A stock dividend is the issuance of additional shares of stock to investors. These shares may be either newly created or existing shares that the organization purchased in the trading market.

Dividend discount model
The dividend discount model is used to determine if a stock is overvalued or undervalued. This is done by predicting the amount of dividends to be paid over the holding period of the stock and discounting this income flow to the present value. If the number obtained by the dividend discount model is higher than what the stock is currently trading at, then the stock is undervalued. This may mean that the stock is a good investment and that there is the potential for capital gains. This model is only used on stocks that pay a regular dividend.

Methods to determine dividend policy
The three common methods by which companies establish a dividend policy are as follows:
- Stability—As the name implies, the policy is one in which a consistent payout ratio is established, usually as a percentage of earnings or a fixed amount per share, in order to provide certainty of income to shareholders and potential investors.
- Residual—This approach coordinates the dividend policy with capital budgeting and the ratio of debt to equity. Dividends are paid only if sufficient equity is available after all capital projects are funded and in an amount that conforms with the desired capital structure as measured by the debt to equity ratio.
- Hybrid—This approach establishes a stable dividend payout in an amount that can consistently maintained regardless of business cycle fluctuations coupled with a residual amount paid only when sufficient earnings are available.

Arguments in favor of and against paying dividends

Arguments in favor of dividend payouts include the following:

- Shareholders (and potential investors) receive a consistent stream of income, thus enhancing the perceived value of the stock as an investment.
- The consistent payment of dividends is thought to create a positive impression of a company by investors, indicating financial strength and effective management.
- Capital asset pricing models include dividends as a component of the valuation equation.

Arguments opposed to dividend payouts include the following:

- Long-term returns to shareholders are enhanced by retaining funds otherwise paid as dividends in order to increase the resources available for reinvestment in the company.
- Funds that cannot be reinvested (due to a lack of opportunities with sufficient returns) are best used to repurchase outstanding shares (thus increasing the value of holdings for each shareholder) rather than paid as dividends.
- Dividend policies, once established, are extremely difficult to reduce or discontinue due to unfavorable shareholder (and market) reaction.

Dividend payout ratio and dividend yield

The dividend payout ratio is the mechanism that determines the amount of earnings, retained or current, that are available for payment of dividends. It is typically calculated as either the dividends paid per share divided by earnings per share or, simply, dividends paid divided by net income. The residual earnings amount after dividends are paid is known as the retention ratio (calculated as 1 minus the payout ratio). The dividend yield is the measurement of the return provided to investors on their holdings of the stock of a company. In effect, it is a static measure of the return on investment in a stock (static because it ignores a growth factor) and is calculated as the dividends paid per share divided by the share price.

Retained earnings

Retained earnings are those earnings of a corporation that are not paid out in dividends. Retained earnings are also called undistributed profits, retention ratio, earned surplus, or retained surplus. Retained earnings are kept by the corporation for future growth or to repay debt. Retained earnings are recorded in a balance sheet account under shareholders' equity. To compute retained earnings, take the retained earnings for the beginning of the accounting period, add net income, and subtract dividends paid. If the corporation experiences operating losses, retained earnings will be reduced and the retained earnings account may have a negative balance. If the corporation declares a stock dividend, retained earnings will be reduced and capital stock will increase. The determining factors as to whether earnings should be retained by the corporation include the tax treatment of the dividends and funds needed for reinvestment in the corporation.

Debt securities

A debt security is an investment that takes the form of a loan taken out by an issuer (who may be a corporation, municipality, government agency, or national government). The person or organization that gives the loan (provides the investment funds) is the investor.

In exchange for the funds, the issuer pays interest on the debt and repays the original loan amount at a specified time in the future. Examples of debt securities are bills, corporate bonds, municipal bonds, treasury bonds, commercial paper, and treasury notes. Debt securities that offer a higher rate of interest are riskier than those that offer a lower interest rate. Investors of debt securities do not have the same rights as investors of equity securities. The holder of the debt securities only has a claim against the issuer as specified by the indenture, but no ownership rights.

Advantages and disadvantages
Debt securities allow the issuer to raise capital to finance capital projects without sacrificing ownership in the organization. Debt securities add liquidity to the balance sheet by converting balance sheet assets (such as mortgages, leases, receivables) into marketable securities. Debt securities pay a fixed interest rate and when interest rates are going up, the price of the debt will go down. If the organization or government that issues the bond has cash flow problems or files for bankruptcy, the investor may not realize interest payments and the issuer may default on the debt.

Valuation
The first valuation criteria is the interest rate paid by the debt security. This depends on the current market interest rate, the term length of the debt, and the credit rating of the issuer. After a debt security has been issued, the market value of the debt security may change. To compensate for market fluctuations, debt securities are priced in terms of percentage of par value. Par value is 100% of the face value of the debt. Some debt securities are issued at a discount and pay the par value at maturity. The market value of the debt security is calculated as the present value of all future interest and principal payments discounted at the yield or rate of return of the debt security. There is an inverse relationship between debt security yield and price. When market interest rates rise, debt security prices usually fall.

Equity securities

An equity security is an investment that represents ownership in a corporation and gives the shareholder a claim to the corporation's earnings and assets. The shareholder is an owner in the corporation. The percentage of ownership depends on the number of shares of stock the shareholder holds. There are two basic types of equity securities: common stock and preferred stock. Owners of common stock have the right to vote at shareholders' meetings and to receive dividends. Owners of preferred stock do not vote at shareholders' meetings and receive dividends before common shareholders. In addition, if the corporation is dissolved, liquidated, or goes bankrupt, preferred shareholders have priority over common shareholders in the distribution of assets.

Market value method

The market value method is used to record equity and debt securities at market value at the end of an accounting period. The market value method is used by an investor who own less than 20% of an equity position in a corporation. This method is used for trading and available-for-sale securities. Trading securities are current assets because they are held for a short period of time and are easily converted to cash. Available-for-sale securities are noncurrent assets. The gain or loss on these investments is calculated by subtracting the cost of the security from the market value of the security. The unrealized gain or loss for trading securities is reported on the income statement. The unrealized gain or loss for available-for-sale securities is reported as other comprehensive income on the income statement and the cumulative amount is reported on the balance sheet in the shareholders' equity section.

Discounted cash flow methods to value stocks and bonds

Discounted cash flow is a method to project the potential future income of an investment in terms of its present value. This is done by determining what the future cash flow or income may be and discounting it for the time value of money to arrive at a present value. This method determines whether an investment will be profitable or not. If the discounted cash flow is higher than the current cost of the investment, the investment may be profitable to the investor.

Derivatives

Derivatives are used to manage the risk of fluctuating interest rates, exchange rates, and commodity prices. They are used to increase the change of a return on investment when these risks are a consideration. A derivative can be either a forward contract, a futures contract, an option, or a swap.

Price/Earnings, Price/Book, and Price/Sales ratios

The Price/Earnings ratio is the ratio of the market price of a common stock divided by its earnings per share. It is used to compare the current earnings on common stock to its predicted future earnings. The Price/Earnings ratio is an estimate of how much an investor is paying for a corporation's future earnings. The higher the Price/Earnings ratio, the higher the earning potential of the stock. The Price/Book ratio is the stock's market price divided by its book value. The Price/Book ratio determines whether a stock is undervalued or overvalued. The Price/Sales ratio is the stock price divided by its per-share sales. This ratio determines whether the current market price of the stock is overpriced or underpriced.

Black-Scholes model

The Black-Scholes model shows the variation of the price of an investment over a period of time. This model is used to predict the price of European put and call options on stocks that do not pay a dividend. This model uses the stock's price variation, the time value of money, the option's strike price, and the option's expiration date to predict the price of the option. It is one of the best ways to determine if an option is priced fairly.

Future contract and forward contract

A future contract is a financial instrument that allows a buyer to purchase an investment or a seller to sell an investment in the future at a predetermined date and price. A future contract is used when speculating on the price of the investment. By purchasing a future contract, risk can be reduced. A forward contract is where an investment is not delivered until a future date but the price is determined at the date the forward contract is made. Forward contracts are usually made by the manufacturer of a product (such as a farmer) who wants a guaranteed price for the product.

Cost of capital

Cost of capital is the debt and equity that an organization invests in a major financing project. A project may include building a manufacturing plant or upgrading manufacturing equipment. In order for an organization to finance a project, the rate of return on the cost of capital needs to be determined. The ability of the organization to raise financing and how the financing will be made depends on this rate of return. Methods of financing may include issuing stock (equity financing) or borrowing (debt financing). For a project to be profitable, the rate of return must be greater than the cost of capital.

Binomial option-valuation model

The binomial option-valuation model is a method to value options based on the time between the valuation date of the option and the expiration date of the option. This model makes it easier to reduce risk by reducing the possibility of price changes and arbitrage. It assumes that the financial market is efficient. It is used on options which can be exercised at any time during the option contract period.

Capital structure

The capital structure is the way an organization is financed. Usually, financing methods are equity financing (common and preferred stock) or debt financing (loans and bonds). The capital structure determines the investment risk of an organization. This risk is determined by the organization's debt-to-equity ratio. An organization that has more debt financing than equity financing is a higher risk than an organization that has a higher amount of equity financing over debt financing.

Cost of debt and cost of equity

Cost of debt is the rate of non-defaulting bonds that have the same duration period of the debt incurred by the organization. Added to this rate is a premium which depends on the amount of debt incurred. Cost of debt is an after tax cost and is discounted by the tax rate paid by the organization. Cost of equity is the expected return on equity based on market interest rates. The expected return is the dividend per share divided by the price per share plus the expected growth rate of the dividend.

Advantages and disadvantages of debt financing

Debt financing has the advantage of allowing the owners of an organization to retain their percentage share of ownership and their percentage share of profits. Debt financing does not require that any part of the organization's assets be sold in order to obtain financing. Debt financing also has a limited risk period which is limited to the repayment period of the debt. Once the debt is repaid, the debt holder no longer has any claim on the organization. The disadvantages are that the loan and interest must be repaid which can be a burden on cash flow. Also, a small company or a newly established company may not have the credit history to qualify for debt financing.

Advantages and disadvantages of equity financing

The advantages of equity financing are that it is easier for small business to obtain money to build the business and there is no obligation to repay the investment. In addition, people who supply equity financing may also be a source of advice and help to small businesses that require this type of financing. The disadvantages are that the owners of an organization that uses equity financing will have to give up a percentage of ownership and control to obtain the equity financing. In addition, equity financing is difficult to administer and may require legal and accounting fees to do the necessary paperwork to comply with securities regulations.

Working capital

Working capital is the total current assets of a corporation less its current liabilities. Working capital is the amount of assets a corporation can convert into cash in the short term (one year or less). This is a measure of a corporation's liquidity and the amount of cash that will need to be used to meet its obligations. When there is an increase in working capital, a corporation has increased the amount of liquid resources over the year and subsequently has increased the inflow of funds. When there is a decrease in working capital, the corporation is using more liquid resources than it is creating. To make decisions based on working capital, a statement of changes in financial position should be compiled. The states of changes show the changes in working capital due to borrowing or financing, selling capital stock, selling an asset, and selling inventory.

Weighted average cost of capital

Weighted average cost of capital is a measurement of an organization's cost of capital in each category of capital. The categories of capital are common stock, preferred stock, bonds, and long-term debt. To compute the weighted average cost of capital multiply each category of capital by its proportional weight and then add these figures together. The value applied to the category of capital is its market value. This figure shows how much an organization pays for each dollar financed either by debt or equity. It also helps management decide if it should undertake an expansion in the business or consider a merger.

Cash

Cash is legal tender than can be used to purchase goods, services, and repay debt. Cash includes paper currency and coins, money orders, checks, accounts at financial institutions, cash equivalents, and marketable securities. Cash equivalents are investments that are highly liquid and safe. Cash equivalents have a known market value and a maturity of less than three months. Examples of cash equivalents are money market accounts and treasury bills. Marketable securities are investments that are liquid and have a maturity of less than one year. These securities can be sold at a price that closely equals their purchase price. Marketable securities include commercial paper, money market investments, banker's acceptances, and government bonds. Cash is carried as a current asset account on an organization's balance sheet. All cash items are carried on the balance sheet at the lower of cost or market value.

Cash flow

Cash flow is the change in the amount of cash held by an organization as a result of cash received (inflow) and cash spent (outflow). Cash inflow comes from operations, financing, and investing. Cash outflow is the result of expenses paid or investments made. Cash flow is an indication of an organization's financial solvency and liquidity. It is essential to manage cash flow so that an organization will have enough cash on hand to pay its creditors and employees. If these obligations cannot be made, the organization may become insolvent which could lead to bankruptcy. When an organization has excess cash flow, it is able to use this extra money to invest in the business and increase potential profits.

Concentration banking and compensating balance

Concentration banking is used by an organization to facilitate the processing of customer payments when the organization sells its product in various states or countries. The organization will select a bank in each geographical area to which customers in that geographical area will send their payments. Once funds are collected, each bank will transfer the balance of the organization's account to the organization's main banking account. A compensating balance is an interest payment that is deducted immediately when an organization takes out a loan. This interest payment is a percentage of the loan. A compensating balance has the effect of increasing the interest rate paid on the loan.

Lockbox system

A lockbox is a box at a U. S. Post Office that is used to collect bill payments from customers. An organization will set up a lockbox to which customers send their payments. These payments are then collected by the organization's bank, the monies processed, and then deposited into the organization's account. The bank also provides the organization with a list of the customers who made payments and the amounts received from each customer. From this list, the organization can update its accounts receivable records. The use of a lockbox can expedite getting money into the organization's banking accounts, help improve cash flow, and reduce processing float. A lockbox system also has the benefit of being a lower cost method of collecting customer funds especially when payments are of a high dollar amount and a low number of transactions.

Disbursement float and overdraft systems

Float is the amount of time that elapses between the time a check is written and when it is presented to the bank which holds the checking account. The funds from the disbursing checking account are not deducted when the check is written. The funds are disbursed when the check is presented to the bank. The writer of the check has use of the funds between the time the check is written and the time it is presented for payment at the bank. An overdraft system allows the writer of a check to write checks on an account which does not have adequate funds to cover the amount of the check. In most instances, the bank that honors the overdraft will charge the account holder a fee or interest for providing this service.

Drafts and zero balance accounts to pay accounts payable

A draft is an order from one person or organization to another stating that they will pay a certain amount of money in exchange for goods or services purchased. The person who receives the draft only has to present the draft to the maker's bank to collect payment. A draft may be made payable immediately or payment may be made some time in the future. A draft is a legal obligation to pay the amount stated on the draft. A zero balance account is a checking account that does not maintain a monetary balance. When checks are presented for payment against the account, money is transferred from another account for the amount of the checks presented.

Marketable securities

Marketable securities are also called temporary investments. Marketable securities are any investment that is held by an organization for a short term which is usually less than a year. Marketable securities are also easily and quickly converted into cash. Usually, marketable securities take the form of bonds and stocks. An organization would invest in marketable securities when it has excess cash that is not needed for current day-to-day operations. This excess cash can be put to better use by being invested so that the cash returns a profit. Marketable securities are also used when an organization has a widely fluctuating cash flow during the year. When the cash flow is high, excess cash can be invested until the cash is needed during low cash flow periods.

Electronic commerce

Electronic commerce (or e-commerce) is selling goods and services over the Internet. This process involves building a presence on the Internet by designing Web pages where customers can browse products through an online catalog. When a customer sees a product they wish to purchase, they can add this item to their shopping cart. When they are ready to pay for their purchases, they checkout and provide the organization with a method of payment. This payment method is usually by credit card. Other payment methods are by electronic check or a bill paying service. Other forms of electronic commerce include disseminating company or product information, finding new markets and customers for a product, and to provide customer service. Electronic commerce is gaining popularity because it is a less expensive and time consuming method of selling products and servicing customers.

Accounts receivable

Accounts receivable are monies owed to an organization by its customers who have purchased products or services, have received those products or services, but have not yet paid for the products or services. Organizations grant credit to its customers with the understanding that the money owed will be paid back within a short period of time. This period of time may range from a few days to as long as a year. Customers are granted credit for a variety of reasons including frequency of purchases and ability to repay the amount owed. Accounts receivable are recorded on the balance sheet as a current asset. When the account receivable is incurred, the account receivable account is debited and the revenue account is credited. When the account receivable is paid, the account receivable is credited and cash is debited. The disadvantage to carrying accounts receivable is when customers do not pay on their accounts when due. When this happens, the organization is not only unable to collect money due it, it is unable to pay its bills (accounts payable) and expenses.

Accounts receivable are monies due to an organization from purchasers of their products but not collected from these purchasers. This is a method of extending credit to customers. Before an organization will allow a customer to set up a credit account, the customer must prove their creditworthiness. These credit accounts must be paid within a short period of time, usually within a few months. Accounts receivable have the advantage of allowing customers to make many purchases but only to make one payment. An account receivable is an asset for the organization because it represents a legal obligation by the customer to pay the organization and the organization can show the account receivable as future cash flow. If an organization has problems collecting on its accounts receivable, it may have difficulties paying its bills.

Collateral
The process of using accounts receivable as collateral is called assignment of accounts receivable. This is accomplished by writing a promissory note to a lender. The organization that borrows the money does not turn over the accounts receivable to the lender. Instead, if the organization is not able to repay the money, the lender can collect the money owed from the accounts receivable as they are paid. Factoring occurs when an organization sells its accounts receivable to another firm. The firm that purchases the accounts receivable pays the organization an agreed upon price. This price is usually at a discount on the total amount of accounts receivable. It is up to the factoring firm to collect the accounts receivable from the organization's customers.

Cash discounts

A cash discount is a reduction in the purchase price of a product or service if the payment is made within a specified period of time. Some cash discounts are given if the product or service is paid at the time of the purchase. Some cash discounts are given if an account receivable is paid before the due date. This is sometimes called a trade credit. Some trade credits on accounts receivable take the form 2% 10 days net 30. This means that if the account is paid within 10 days, the customer may take a 2% discount off of the amount due. If the account is not paid within 10 days, then the full amount is due in 30 days. The advantage of using cash discounts is that the seller does not have as long to wait before payment is received.

Default risk

Default risk is a risk that a debtholder undertakes when loaning money to a debtor. The risk is that the debtor will not make the principal and interest payments on the loan when these payments are due. Default risk can be determined by looking at an individual's or at an organization's credit rating. The higher the credit rating, the less likely the debtor will default on the loan and thereby reduces the risk.

Imputed interest

Imputed interest is assumed interest. It is the interest that the borrower would pay on a debt instrument in a normal transaction if the debt instrument used a market interest rate. Some debt types either have no interest payment or have a very low interest payment.

These debt types include non-interest bearing notes, discounted debts, and zero-coupon instruments. On a non-interest bearing note, an assumed interest rate will need to be calculated. The interest amount is then deducted from the principal amount of the note to determine the principal portion of the note. For example, on a one year $1000 note with a 10% simple interest rate, the interest would be $100 and the principal amount would be $900.

Uncollectible accounts

Uncollectible accounts are any type of receivable account, such as accounts receivable and notes receivable, which has the possibility of not being paid. These types of accounts may not be paid because the customer who owes the money is having cash flow problems, is going bankrupt, or has another reason for defaulting on the receivable account. Many organizations make allowances for uncollectible accounts in their accounting records. This is done by determining the percentage of its accounts that become uncollectible during the average year. Then, the organization multiplies this percentage to its accounts receivable amount. This amount is then debited to a bad debt reserve account and credited to an allowance for bad debts account. When a customer does not pay its accounts receivable, the allowance for bad debts account is debited and the accounts receivable account is credited.

Recourse financing and nonrecourse financing

When an organization factors its accounts receivable, it has one of two options. It can select a factoring firm that provides recourse financing or a factoring firm that provides nonrecourse financing. In recourse financing, the organization is responsible for the debt if its customers cannot pay the amount owed in the accounts receivable. In nonrecourse financing, the factoring firm takes the risk if the customer us unable to pay. If a customer does not make payment, the factoring firm cannot go back to the organization to collect the debt. In recourse financing, the organization will pay lower fees to the factoring firm and pay a lower discount rate thereby receiving more money for their accounts receivable. This is because the organization takes on the majority of the risk and the risk to the factoring firm is reduced.

Lead time and safety stock

Lead time is the time that elapses between the start of a project and its completion. When manufacturing a product, it is the amount of time that is needed from the time raw materials are ordered until these raw materials are received and are able to be incorporated into the manufacturing process. Safety stock is an amount of inventory that an organization carries above an amount that is necessary to meet production schedules and to fill customer orders. Safety stock is carried when an organization is not sure about the demand for their product or is unsure if they will be able to order needed raw materials.

Inventory

Inventory is the value of the raw materials, work in progress, supplies used in operations, and finished goods held by an organization. Inventory is valued based on the lower of the cost to produce or the current market price. The purpose of inventory is to ensure that an organization will be able to provide its customers with product when the customer demands the product. Inventory requires a cash investment in product and storage. When an organization holds too much inventory, there is the risk that demand for the product will go down or disappear. This would leave the organization with product that it cannot sell. Other risks include loss due to theft, damage, or obsolescence. A major factor in determining an organization's financial condition is inventory turnover. Inventory turnover is the rate at which products are turned into cash.

Carrying inventory

Inventory is a supply of products or materials that an organization keeps on hand to manufacture a product or to deliver a product to its customers. Organizations carry inventory to ensure that all sales to customers are filled. Holding inventory in storage costs an organization money, time, and profits. For these reasons, an organization needs to plan and forecast its inventory needs and the needs of its customers. There are risks associated with carrying inventory. If there is a change in customer needs, an organization may find itself with product that it can no longer sell. Also, inventory is subject to risks outside the control of the organization such as fire, flood, and theft. The benefits of carrying inventory must be weighed against the risks of carrying inventory to determine the optimal level of inventory.

Types of inventory

The three inventory types are raw materials, work in progress, and finished goods. Raw materials are the materials and other components that are scheduled for use in the making of a final product. Examples of raw materials are cloth that is being held so that it can be turned into clothing, and steel that is being held for use in the making of automobiles. Work in progress is the materials and other components that are in the process of being turned into a final product. Examples of work in progress is cloth that has been cut into pieces and is ready to be assembled into clothing, and steel parts that are ready to be assembled into the final automobile. Finished goods are those final products that are ready to be sold to customers. Examples of finished goods are the clothing that is packaged and ready for sale, and the automobile that is sitting on the dealer showroom.

Inventory accounting and valuation

Inventory is recorded as a current asset on the balance sheet of an organization. The method used to value the inventory is a determining factor in the total assets of the organization. On the income statement, inventory valuation affects cost of goods sold, gross profit margin, net income before taxes, taxes owed, and net income. There are several approaches to valuing inventory – the specific identification method, first-in first-out, and last-in first-out. The inventory valuation method is a matter of choice for an organization. Because of this, it is imperative that any analysis of the financial statements of the organization include an understanding of the inventory footnote. This footnote details the method of inventory valuation used by the organization.

LIFO inventory method: Last-in, first-out (LIFO)is an inventory accounting method where those products that have been in inventory the shortest amount of time are the first products to be sold out of inventory. If the inventory item is sold for more than its cost of production, there is a gain. If the inventory item is sold for less that its cost of production, there is a loss. The last-in, first-out method is a disadvantage to organizations during periods of rising prices. When the sales price of a product has increased, selling recent inventory items results in a higher cost of goods sold and a lower profit margin. The advantage is that it results in a lower taxable income. LIFO cushion results during inflationary periods because the inventory valuation is artificially low.

- 42 -

FIFO inventory method: First-in, first-out (FIFO) is an inventory accounting method where those products that have been in inventory the longest are the first products to be sold out of inventory. In other words, the inventory is sold in chronological order. In the first-in, first-out method, ending inventory is valued at the current cost. The first-in, first-out method is advantageous to organizations during periods of rising prices. When the sales price of a product has increased, selling older inventory items results in a lower cost of goods sold and a higher profit margin. The disadvantage is that it also results in a higher taxable income.

Tracking inventory

Inventory is tracked using one of two systems – the continuous review system and the periodic review system. In the continuous review system, an organization keeps a running total of the amount of inventory by logging each inventory item as it is put into inventory and as it is sold. In this system, when the inventory level reaches a predetermined level, the organization will place more products into inventory to return the inventory level to the desired amount. The continuous review system is also referred to as event triggered systems, fixed order size systems, and economic order quantity systems. In the periodic review system, the inventory level is counted at specified periodic intervals. The inventory may be counted weekly, monthly, quarterly, or yearly. The periodic review system is also referred to as fixed order interval systems and economic order interval systems.

Economic Order Quantity

Economic Order Quantity is the optimum amount of raw material or product that an organization should order for its inventory to minimize the costs of obtaining that inventory. These costs can include holding costs, order costs, and shortage costs. Economic Order Quantity is method used to maintain an optimum inventory system. Economic Order Quantity assumes that an organization knows the demand and lead time of the product, that there are not quantity discounts, and that shortages do not occur. By ordering the optimum quantity when inventory levels reach a certain minimum level, an organization can ensure that it will have adequate inventory to meet its customer's needs. This guarantees that customer orders will not go unfilled. It also ensures that an organization will not use up needed working capital on inventory that sits in its storage facility for long periods of time.

F.o.b.

Free on board (f.o.b.) is a term used when shipping products in a vessel such as a ship or a truck. In this shipping arrangement, the shipper delivers the product onto the vessel. There are two arrangements that can be made – f.o.b. shipping point and f.o.b. destination. Free on board means that the shipper makes delivery without charge. When the free on board designation is a shipping point, the seller is responsible for the product and the cost of shipping until the seller delivers the product to the carrier (the ship or truck). Once the product in on the carrier, it is no longer the seller's responsibility. The seller then invoices the purchaser for the product and the cost to move the product to the shipping point. When the free on board designation is a destination, the seller is responsible for the product and the cost of shipping until the product reaches the specified destination (which is usually the purchaser's place of business). Title to the product passes from the seller to the purchaser at the f.o.b. point.

Trade credit

Trade credit is credit extended from one business to another when goods or services are purchased. In most instances, the business that extends the credit allows the purchasing business as long as three months to repay the debt. As an incentive to repay the debt sooner than three months, the business extending the credit may offer a discount for prompt payment. A business may request trade credit to delay payments for purchases such as inventory items, materials needed to manufacture goods, or seasonal products. This may be necessary because of the delay between the time of purchase and the time when the business may be able to sell the product. The payment is delayed so that repayment is not made until the business can collect revenues from the sale of the product financed. Trade credit in this instance is a way to provide the business with working capital.

Current liability

A current liability is a debt or obligation that an organization expects to pay off within one year. Current liabilities are incurred by an organization in the course of normal, day to day operations. In most instances, cash or other current assets are used to pay current liabilities. Current liabilities appear on an organization's balance sheet as a sub-category of liabilities. Examples of current liabilities include accounts payable, short-term loans, accrued expenses payable, and the portion of long-terms loans that are due in one year. The amount of an organization's working capital is an important indication of an organization's ability to continue business operations. Working capital is calculated by subtracting total current liabilities from total current assets. The determination of the ability of an organization to be able to pay off its current liabilities is the current ratio and the quick ratio. The current ratio is current assets divided by current liabilities. The quick ratio is current assets minus inventories, divided by current liabilities.

Bankers' acceptance

A bankers' acceptance is a short-term method of financing where a bank issues a draft on behalf of its customer. The bank guarantees that the draft will be paid on a specified date. A bank acts in the good faith that their customer will realize income from the goods purchased by the loan at some point in the future. If the borrower does not repay the loan, the bank will pay the amount due. Bankers' acceptances are usually extended from 30 to 180 days. Bankers' acceptances are usually used to facilitate international trade. If an organization is unknown by the foreign seller, the bank will use its reputation to help the organization finance the goods it desires to purchase from the foreign seller.

Commercial paper

Commercial paper is a short-term method of financing accounts receivable, inventory, production, and other short term liabilities. Commercial paper cannot be issued to finance fixed assets. An organization issues unsecured notes that can be traded in the public money market. These notes are unsecured because they are not guaranteed by any collateral. Commercial paper has a term of less than 270 days. When commercial paper is issued, it is usually sold at a discount which is determined by the current interest rates. The interest paid on commercial paper is usually lower than the rate an organization would have to pay to a bank for a short term loan. An organization can issue commercial paper without filing any paperwork with regulatory agencies such as the Securities and Exchange Commission.

- 44 -

Secured credit

Secured credit is a loan that uses an asset as collateral. The lender is guaranteed payment even if the borrower defaults, at which time the lender may take possession of the collateral. The collateral is usually an asset such as real estate, machinery, or a banking account. If the borrower defaults on the loan, the lender becomes the owner of the asset and may sell the asset to recover the loan amount. The lender assumes less risk when making the loan because of the collateral pledged by the borrower. Secured credit may also be obtained at a lower rate because of this reduced risk.

Line of credit

A line of credit is a borrowing limit that a bank will extend to a customer. The customer can use this credit to finance any of its needs at any time it chooses. A line of credit may or may not have any repayment period. Although, a bank will stipulate that when the customer reaches the limit of the line of credit that the indebtedness be repaid before additional credit will be extended. The customer may elect to repay the line of credit in full or it may make a partial payment.

Use of factoring in inventory financing

Factoring is used when an organization obtains accounts receivable financing that is in excess of its accounts receivable. The excess amount of the loan is applied against the organization's inventory. It is assumed that this excess amount will be repaid out of the future sales of the inventory. The lender that factors the accounts receivable becomes the owner of the accounts receivable. This means that if the customers default on their accounts receivable payments, the lender cannot go back to the organization and collect the debt. The lender assumes additional risk in this type of arrangement.

Accounts receivable financing

Accounts receivable financing occurs when an organization uses its accounts receivable as collateral for a loan. The loan amount is usually limited by the dollar value of the accounts receivable and the amount of time the organization has held the accounts receivable. The longer the organization has held the accounts receivable the less they will receive for the loan. This is because of the risk of not being able to collect on the aged accounts receivable. Accounts receivable financing is a way for an organization to obtain working capital quicker than it can collect on its accounts receivable. When the accounts receivable are financed, the organization no longer has the responsibility for collecting on these accounts. The responsibility for collecting the accounts receivable is with the creditor. This gives the organization more time to focus on its business activities by not having to spend time collecting monies due.

SEC

The Securities and Exchange Commission (SEC) was formed as a result of the Securities Exchange Act of 1934 for the purposes of providing for the protection of investors; providing for and maintaining orderly and efficient markets; and the facilitation of capital formation, issuance and exchange. The responsibilities of the SEC include the following:
- Interpretation and enforcement of federal securities laws.
- Securities rule issuance and amendment.
- Inspection of securities industry firms and ratings agencies.
- Oversight of other regulatory organizations with responsibility for securities, accounting, and auditing.
- Coordination with federal, state, and other country agencies.

The SEC is governed by five commissioners, each appointed by the president with the advice and consent of the Senate.

FINRA

Financial Industry Regulatory Authority (FINRA) is a not-for-profit, non-stock corporation owned by its members, who are dealers, brokers, and other investment banking-related entities that, collectively, constitute the securities industry. As such, FINRA provides for and administers the self-regulation of the industry as a national securities association authorized by the Securities Exchange Act of 1934. The mission of FINRA includes the following:
- Promotion of the industry, standardization of principles and practices, and promotion of high commercial honor and integrity.
- Coordination and cooperation with governmental and other agencies.
- Promotion of equitable principles and practices of fair trade and rigorous investor protection.
- Promotion of member self-discipline and adjudication of grievances between members and investors.

CFTC and NFA

The Commodity Futures Trading Commission (CFTC) was created as a result of the Commodities Exchange Act (CEA) of 1936 and serves as its primary regulatory body. It is the responsibility of the CFTC to regulate the actions of commodities traders engaged in trading futures contracts, options on futures contracts, options on physical commodities, security futures products, and some retail foreign exchange contracts. Section 17 of the CEA provides for the registration of industry self-regulating organizations with the CFTC to operate in a regulatory role over the actions of its members.

The National Futures Association (NFA) is the only such organization currently registered and acts on behalf of the CFTC. The NFA is responsible for the following regulatory functions:
- Auditing and surveillance of NFA members for the purpose of enforcement of compliance with NFA financial requirements.
- Establishment and enforcement of rules and standards in order to ensure customer protection.

- 46 -

- Administration and maintenance of an arbitration process to adjudicate disputes arising from futures and foreign exchange transactions.
- Determination of fitness of applicants for membership and review of continuing membership for existing members.

Sarbanes-Oxley Act of 2002 and PCAOB

The Sarbanes-Oxley Act of 2002 is also known as the Public Company Accounting Reform and Investor Protection Act of 2002. The Act was put into law to protect investors from fraudulent accounting activities by publicly traded corporations. The Sarbanes-Oxley Act accomplished many goals. The Act established the Public Company Accounting Oversight Board that is the registrar for public companies. The Act implemented the regulation of auditors of publicly traded corporations and required the use of auditing committees and inspecting accounting firms. The Act increased corporate responsibility for fraudulent actions. The Act imposed disclosure guidelines in corporate financial statements. The Act spelled out guidelines to prevent conflicts of interest. The Act also legislated the enforcement of penalties for criminal activities.

The Sarbanes-Oxley Act of 2002 was intended to enhance existing securities regulation in order to mitigate fraudulent accounting practices by public companies. The act, known as SOX, has a number of provisions but is popularly known for the following two key requirements:
- Certification, under penalty of criminal action, of the accuracy of the financial statements of a company by certain officers.
- A requirement that the internal controls and related business processes of a company be documented and certified as accurate by a registered public accounting firm.

PCAOB

The Public Company Accounting Oversight Board (PCAOB) is a five member board that oversees the audits of publicly traded corporation financial statements. Such oversight includes the following responsibilities:
- Registration of public accounting firms that prepare audits subject to SOX compliance.
- Establishment of audit, quality control, ethics, independence, and other standards.
- Inspection of registered public accounting firms.
- Investigations and administration of disciplinary proceedings.

This board ensures that corporate officers certify the accuracy of financial statements and that they report on the effectiveness of internal financial reporting controls. The Public Company Accounting Oversight Board put a ban on loans to corporate executives and directors. It also required companies to institute procedures to handle complaints about accounting and auditing practices.

Auditor requirements for control disclosures
The Public Company Accounting Oversight Board has addressed several areas where auditors need to disclose information about a company's financial statements. The auditor is responsible for assessing the design and operating effectiveness of internal financial

- 47 -

controls. The auditor must understand how transactions are initiated, processed, and reported in the financial records of the company. The auditor must disclose any areas in the financial accounting system where material misstatements may occur. The auditor must evaluate the controls the company has put in place to prevent and detect fraud. The auditor must ensure the accuracy of the financial reporting process. The auditor must ensure that assets are safeguarded. The auditor must also assess the adequacy of the management's assurance that there is an internal control system in place to ensure the accuracy of financial reporting.

Securities Exchange Act of 1934

The Securities Exchange Act of 1934 was enacted to regulate the securities industry, the stock exchanges, securities broker-dealers, and others who worked in the industry. It made it mandatory for public companies to disclose financial and other information. It also enacted regulations for public companies to include corporate governance, tender offers, and proxy solicitations. The Securities Exchange Act of 1934 was the basis for the formation of the Securities and Exchange Commission. The SEC is the federal agency responsible for overseeing the securities markets and enforcing the federal securities laws.

Securities Act of 1933

The Securities Act of 1933 was a result of the securities market crash of 1929. The Act was put into law because there was a need for legislation regarding the sale of securities and a need to regulate the securities markets. After the crash of 1929, the federal government was compelled to bring stability to the securities markets and regain the confidence of investors in the securities market system. The goals of the Act were to make financial statements uniform to help investors make informed decisions about investments and to prevent misrepresentation and fraud in the securities markets. The Act required companies to register their securities with the Securities and Exchange Commission prior to a public sale of the securities. It required companies to disclose to the SEC and the investor community financial information about the company and the stock the company was offering for sale.

Reporting requirement of public companies
Public companies are required by the Securities Act of 1933 to register all sales of securities with the Securities and Exchange Commission. This registration process includes the filing of a registration statement and a prospectus. The prospectus is a disclosure statement that lists all the material facts about the securities being offered for sale and the company issuing the securities. These documents must include pertinent information about the company including a description of the company's properties and business, a description of the security to be offered for sale, information about the company's management, and financial statements that have been certified by an independent accountant.

External financial reporting

External financial reporting consists of providing financial statements to people and organizations that are not directly affiliated with an organization. A financial statement is a report that contains financial information about an organization. These financial statements include the balance sheet, income statement, statement of cash flows, statement of changes in financial position, statement of stockholders' equity, and statement of comprehensive income. If the organization is a publicly held company, it is required by the Securities and

Exchange Commission (SEC) to make audited financial statements available to the agency and to its shareholders. When financial statements are prepared for external users, the statements follow generally accepted accounting principles (GAAP). The Financial Accounting Standards Board (FASB) sets the GAAP guidelines for the content and format of the financial statements. In addition, the SEC also has legal responsibility for determining the content and reporting requirements of financial statements.

External users

External users are those people who are not affiliated with the operations of an organization but use the organization's financial information for different reasons. Examples of external users are potential and current investors, bankers and lenders, government agencies, media representatives, and the general public. Investors use financial statements to determine if an organization's stock is a worthwhile investment. Investors and financial analysts use financial statements as a basis for making investment decisions. Bankers and lenders look at financial statements before making loans to an organization. These loans may include working capital, long-term loans, and debentures. Government agencies may need to look at an organization's financials to determine the accuracy of its tax returns or to comply with regulatory requirements. Media representatives and the general public use financial statements for a variety of reasons. It may be to find a newsworthy story or to determine if an organization is acting in a socially responsible manner.

Audit

An audit is an examination of the financial records and accounts of an organization to determine the accuracy of the financial information. Audits are normally performed by CPA firms. The auditor of an organization's financial statements must be proficient in accounting and auditing, be independent from the organization, and exercise due professional care. In addition, there must be no financial relationship between the auditor and the organization. During the audit, the auditor must supervise any assistants the auditor brings to the organization to help perform the audit, must understand the organization's internal controls, and must obtain enough evidence to support the information in the financial statements. When compiling the auditor's report, the auditor must ensure that the financial statements met GAAP requirements and report on any change in accounting principles.

Annual report

An annual report is a corporation's annual statement of its financial condition and operations. The annual report is usually published annually. The annual report includes a balance sheet, an income statement, the auditor's reports, and a description of the corporation's operations. Small organizations may only produce an annual report that is no more than a few pages long and only meets the minimum legal requirements. Larger organizations may include more information. The annual report is used by investors, creditors, employees, regulatory agencies, and financial analysts. It is used to determine the financial condition of a corporation and to assess its future plans and growth potential. If the corporation is a publicly traded company, the annual report is submitted to the SEC (in the form of a 10-K) along with more detailed financial information.

Auditor's reports

An auditor can issue five types of reports regarding the soundness of an organization's financial statements – unqualified opinion, unqualified opinion with explanatory language, qualified opinion, adverse opinion, and disclaimer of opinion. The unqualified report is given when the financial statements of the organization fairly represent the financial position of the organization, when the financial statements are prepared according to GAAP, and when the audit complies with GAAS. The unqualified opinion with explanatory language report is used when a situation such as a change in accounting principle does not affect the unqualified opinion. The qualified opinion is given when there is a deviation from GAAP, but this deviation is not material. The adverse opinion is used when the deviation from GAAP is material and the organization will not change its financial statements. A disclaimer of opinion is given when the auditor feels that the deviation from GAAP is so severe that the auditor cannot give an opinion as to the fairness of the financial statements.

10-K filing

The 10-K is an annual report that a publicly traded company files with the Securities and Exchange Commission. This filing contains the same information as reported in the company's annual report along with some extra information. The report includes a description of the industry in which the company conducts business. The audited income statement, statement of financial position, statement of cash flow, and notes to the financial statements are included. The management discussion and analysis of the current financial position of the company and a brief outline of the company's accomplishments over the past two years are added to the financial statements. Information detailing the company's operating segments is added. A list of the company's directors and officers that details the occupation and employer of each director is a part of the report. And, the market price of the company's stock and the dividends paid during the past year are disclosed.

Financial institutions

In general, financial institutions serve as the intermediary between investors and borrowers, facilitating the efficient transfer of capital.

Commercial banking, insurance and pensions, and investments and trading
A commercial bank is an institution, either federally or state chartered, that accepts and manages deposits and makes loans available to borrowers. Other than a bank, such institutions include credit unions, trust companies, mortgage lenders, and building societies. Insurance and pension companies are contractual entities that provide actuarial and risk management services to individuals and companies. An insurance company evaluates various forms of risk and assumes all or a portion of the liability in exchange for premium income. Pension companies manage funds invested for the retirement benefit of groups of individuals. Investment and trading companies are financial institutions that specialize in the securities industry, facilitating merger and acquisition activity and managing the issuance of securities and trading in financial instruments, either on behalf of customers or using in-house capital.

Sources of capital
Commercial banks are the primary source of term loans both unsecured (such as a line of credit) and secured (such as mortgages and asset-based financing). The larger banks also

offer trading services in more exotic instruments, such as swaps and other derivatives. Insurance and pension companies act as a source of capital by investing premium income and employee and employer contributions in various financial instruments. Insurance companies typically invest in high-quality corporate bonds and private debt placements as well as new equity issues and preferred stock. Pension funds are major participants in the equity markets but also have holdings in fixed income and real estate. Investment banking provides capital to companies by arranging deals between the providers of capital and the users. Such deals can involve debt or equity through either public offerings (such as an initial public offering, or IPO) or private placement.

IPO

An initial public offering (IPO) represents the first-ever issuance of stock and sale to the public from a company that, prior to the issuance, was privately owned. As a source of capital, an IPO is intended to provide funds to enable a company to grow and expand or to compensate early private investors for their risk. Investment banks are typically employed to underwrite the process, serving as both advisor to the company and broker to the investors. The investment bankers will recommend the appropriate form and size of the securities and will often act as market maker during the early post-issuance trading period. A company that chooses to engage in an IPO is typically one that is young and entrepreneurial with the founders actively involved in key positions seeking to exploit opportunities or develop new products; however, they have reached limitations in their ability to raise capital in order to fund both current operations and future growth.

Pre-IPO, IPO transaction and issuance, and post-IPO
The pre-IPO phase is typically focused on management and governance as the company begins to transform itself. As a public company, professional management is necessary to provide a credible presence on behalf of the company to the investment community as well as to execute the subsequent strategies. A proper governance structure is required in order to meet the rigorous regulatory and reporting requirements of public companies. The IPO transaction and issuance phase takes place during the period leading to the actual issuance of shares in which the company secures the services of appropriate professional advisors. The objective is to present a credible plan to investors regarding the regulatory requirements, governance, financing, and appropriate capital structure. It is also imperative that the company demonstrate ongoing, successful execution of its strategy. During the post-IPO phase, the company requires critical support from the underwriter (typically an investment banking firm) to facilitate orderly trading and to maintain share price support. Thereafter, the key activity is, again, successful execution of strategy and consistent achievement of financial expectations.

Advantages and disadvantages
The advantages of an IPO include access to new sources of capital (via the public equity markets), lower capital costs, and the opportunity to create a more diversified and potentially optimal capital structure. Public companies are also often viewed as more desirable by professional managers and potential employees. The disadvantages include new and often onerous disclosure and regulatory requirements required of public companies (not the least of which is compliance with Sarbanes-Oxley rules) and the difficulty of consistently meeting the always-demanding expectations of investors. In addition, the cost of preparing and executing the offering is significant, requiring the

services of costly professional services in law, accounting, and finance as well as acting as a drain on in-house company resources.

Secondary offering

As its name implies, a secondary offering is an issuance of shares that takes place subsequent to the initial public offering (IPO). These shares were originally registered as part of the IPO but issued to company insiders, venture funding entities, and large institutional investors. As such, the offering in this case is from those early investors to the general public.

Dilution

Dilution is the term used to describe a reduction in the earnings per share of a company solely as a result of an increase in the number of shares outstanding (i.e., an increase in the ratio due to a higher denominator and an unchanged numerator). Because the shares of a secondary offering are held by early investors as part of an original initial public offering, or IPO (i.e., already issued), the shares outstanding of the company remain unchanged. The offering involves a sale between the early investors and the general public. As there is no change in the number of shares outstanding, there can be no dilution of earnings per share.

Stock repurchase

Companies engage in stock repurchase programs for a number of reasons including the following:
- Shares Undervalued—The perception of the value of a company by investors may lag the results produced by various quantitative models. The management of such a company may seek to support the share price by reducing the number of shares outstanding. In theory, assuming a consistent price multiple and net income, a lower number of shares outstanding will yield an increase in earnings per share and share price.
- Stock as Compensation—Companies that provide compensation to employees that include stock, such as through options or restricted stock units, can offset the dilutive effect of issuing the additional shares by repurchasing existing shares outstanding.
- Dividend Alternative—Companies may view a repurchase plan as a more attractive alternative to the payment of dividends. In such a case, the return to the shareholders due to a higher share price is thought to be of greater value than the return of cash through a dividend payment.

Arguments in favor of stock repurchases include the following:
- The price of remaining shares outstanding will increase or, in times of stress, be maintained at existing levels.
- During periods of severe market declines, the price of repurchasing shares can be nominal and the potential return greater relative to other available investments.
- The return to investors via an increase in share price is more tax efficient than paying dividends as capital gains can be deferred until the shares are sold, while dividends are taxed when received.

Arguments opposed to stock repurchases include the following:
- Purchasing shares consumes cash that can be used more efficiently.
- Companies sufficiently profitable to make available cash for stock repurchases typically have higher share prices (reflecting current financial success). Those who cannot afford to repurchase typically have lower share prices (reflecting financial difficulties). Therefore, repurchase programs have the effect of increasing already higher prices and not increasing lower prices.
- Repurchase programs can mask management deficiencies by increasing earnings per share despite underperformance.

Private placement

A private placement represents an offering of a security for sale that is not intended for the general public (i.e., not a public offering). As a result, such offerings are exempt from the registration requirements of the Securities Act of 1933. Investors qualified to participate in private placements (so-called accredited investors) are generally large institutional firms such as banks, mutual funds, insurance companies, and pension funds but also include high net-worth individuals. A traditional private placement is one in which an intermediary (usually an investment bank) is employed to act as a placement agent, advising the issuer on the structure of the deal and marketing the issue to investors. If the terms of the issue include protection for the investors from adverse price changes, the placement is said to be a structured type.

Advantages and disadvantages
The advantages of a private placement include the following:
- The lack of the Securities and Exchange Commission (SEC) registration requirement reduces the cost of issue.
- Public disclosure of confidential information is avoided.
- As the accredited investors are relatively knowledgeable and limited in numbers, the deal structure can be more complex and sophisticated.
- The types of capital available are greater due to the sophistication of the investors (i.e., options, warrants, convertibles, etc.).

The disadvantages of a private placement include the following:
- The issuance of new shares has a dilutive effect on existing shareholders.
- Deals can be difficult to negotiate as investors can be demanding.
- Significant time can be required of company executives and board members in order to satisfy investor concerns.
- Because the deal is private, valuation issues can be significant (i.e., how to value the cost of the issue).

Leases

Effect of leases on organization's financial statements
A lease is a contract that allows an organization to use a specified piece of property or equipment for a limited period of time in exchange for a specified payment amount. At the end of the lease agreement, the property is returned. The party that owns the property or equipment is the lessor. The party that has use of the property or equipment is the lessee. Leases are used to grant temporary use to real estate, equipment, automobiles, and

household appliances. In a lease, the lessee does not carry the property being leased on their financial records as an asset. Instead, the money paid for the use of the property is recorded as an expense. The lessor carries the property as an asset in their financial records and the money received on the lease is recorded as revenue. The lessor also depreciates or amortizes the property and this amount is recorded as an expense.

Lease financing
A lease is a financial contract between two parties that provides for the use of tangible property owned by one party (the lessor) in exchange for consideration from the other party (the lessee). Implicit in the lease payment is an effective rate of interest rendering the arrangement a type of financing; the lessor acts as the creditor and the lessee the debtor. A lease differs from a leveraged purchase in terms of the transfer of ownership of the underlying property. Ownership is retained by the lessor in a lease arrangement but transferred from the seller to the buyer in a purchase arrangement. Otherwise, the repayment mechanism (periodic payment of principal and interest) is essentially identical between the two contracts.

Operating lease and capital lease
An operating lease is one in which ownership of the property is retained by the lessor. The lessee receives only the right to use the property for the period specified in the lease. Operating leases are treated as expense items in the financial statements of the lessee.

An operating lease will become a capital lease if any one of the following four criteria becomes applicable:
- The term of the lease exceeds 75% of the life of the leased property.
- Ownership of the property is transferred to the lessee at the end of the lease.
- There exists a bargain purchase price option in favor of the lessee upon completion of the lease period.
- The present value of the periodic lease payments exceeds 90% of the fair value of the asset.

A capital lease is recorded as the purchase of an asset subject to a liability on the balance sheet of the lessee. The liability is amortized periodically based upon the term of the lease, and interest expense is recognized accordingly.

Equity method

The equity method is used by investors who own between 20% and 50% of the common stock of a corporation. If an investor has significant influence over a corporation (such as a member of the board of directors) and owns less than 20% of the outstanding stock, that investor may also use the equity method. In the equity method, the investor claims a percentage of the profits of the corporation in their accounting records. This is done by debiting the investment in investee account and crediting the equity in earnings of investee account. A loss by the corporation is recorded by debiting the loss account and crediting the investment in investee account. When dividends are received, cash is debited and the investment in investee account is credited.

Organization structure

An organization or business is a complex operation that requires many individuals to perform various unique tasks. Because of this division of tasks and labor, there must be a plan that details the work to be done and the individual or group responsible for completing the work. A structure is necessary because of the number of personnel required to perform all of the tasks needed to produce a product or provide a service. The organization structure consists of functions, relationships, responsibilities, authorities, and communications between individuals and departments. The purpose of an organization structure is to assign responsibility and authority to the management and employees of an organization. The organization structure is depicted through the use of an organizational chart. This organizational structure resembles an inverted tree shape. The base of the chart is the president and board of directors. The branches of the chart are the departments. From the branches, the individuals within each department are displayed. The organizational chart shows the line of responsibility and accountability between subordinates and supervisors.

There are four types of organization structures – functional organization, matrix organization, line organization, and line-and-staff organization. In a functional organization structure, the structure is based on performance or job function. Departments are created based on the function performed such as accounting, human resources, sales, and purchasing. In a matrix organization, the structure is a mix of performance and project needs. In this structure, members from different departments are brought together to complete a project. A matrix organization may contain a mix of accounting, engineering, and sales personnel. Line organization structures are usually used by smaller organizations. In a line organization structure, the structure is based on a function. In this structure, all of the jobs provided by that function are contained within the line structure. Line-and-staff structures are usually used by larger organizations. In a line-and-staff organization, the functions performed by the organization are outlined and the departments that support these functions are associated with each function.

Functional organization structure
A functional organization structure separates the organization into functional areas instead of by product lines. This allows an organization to group employees with similar skills and who perform a similar task into a separate department or unit. The functional organization structure is most efficient when an organization produces a specific and uniform product. Usually the organization produces a single product or a variety of products that all use a central core. In the functional organization structure, each department or unit becomes specialized and highly efficient at performing their assigned tasks. This type of organization structure does not provide for flexibility and can cause communication difficulties between departments and units.

Line organization structure
A line organization is one of the traditional organization structures. This type of structure uses the various functions or departments as the basis of the structure. The lines of authority at all management levels follow the organization's customs and procedures. In a line organization, there is a clear chain of command and the responsibility for decision making comes from upper or senior management. The line structure is normally used by small organizations. In these organizations, the president or owner oversees the entire organization, directs and manages all employees, and has final decision making authority. In most instances, the president or owner is involved in the day-to-day operations of the

organization, performs many of the same job functions as the employees, and is available to employees to offer assistance and guidance. The line organization has a small number of departments, an informal working atmosphere, and is decentralized.

Matrix organization structure

A matrix organization structure is similar to a line-and-staff organization structure in that the work flow is organized based on a function or a project and employees of various departments support the various projects. The difference is that when an employee is assigned to a project, that employee is managed by their respective department manager (a vertical authority relationship) and the project manager (a horizontal work relationship). Because each employee reports to two managers, management of the matrix organization structure may become difficult. These difficulties arise when there are conflicting roles between what is expected of the employee from the department manager and the project manager, when one manager requires more time and effort from the employee, and when there are conflicting deadlines between the department and the project. The matrix organization structure is centralized, decision making is accomplished faster than in a line-and-staff structure but slower than a line structure, and the work atmosphere is more formal than a line structure but less formal than a line-and-staff structure.

Line-and-staff organization structure

The line-and-staff organization structure is used by larger organizations where many departments are involved in providing services to many different projects or functions. Examples of this are the sales department that provides sales and marketing for many different product lines, the accounting department that keeps financial records for the entire organization, and the information technology department that provides computer services to other departments within the organization. The line-and-staff organization structure combines the line structure, where authority and responsibility lines are based on the work flow, with the departments that support the work flow. Authority over subordinates is the responsibility of the line manager; staff positions do not have any authority over line positions. The line-and-staff organization structure provides a system of checks and balances to ensure that the work flow is efficient and that there is accountability for the end result. Line-and-staff organization structures have a centralized chain of command, a formal working atmosphere, and many departments.

Line authority and staff authority: Line authority is the ability of a manager to give orders to and delegate responsibility to those employees that are direct subordinates. A line manager is responsible for ensuring that an organization's goals are attained and that the employees under the manager's direction perform their jobs efficiently and effectively. Line authority is found in manufacturing and sales departments. Staff authority is the ability of a manager to provide advice, support, and service to the employees of a line department. The staff manager does not have the ability to command employees. Staff functions include planning, organization, and budgeting. Staff authority is found in human resources, purchasing, and accounting departments.

Decentralized structure

An organization with a decentralized structure has fewer management levels than in a centralized structure and provides more decision making authority and control to lower levels of management. Decentralized organizations tend to foster employee creativity and reduce management costs. A decentralized structure also forces management to delegate more work and authority to employees, allows employees to take complaints and concerns directly to upper management, and provides management with a hands-on approach to the daily operations. In a decentralized structure, the chain of command is shortened and the decision making process moves quickly. Decisions are made by the managers responsible for the work and approval is made by that manager's immediate supervisor. This decision making process is performed within the line-and-staff organization where the staff performs the actual work and the line functions manage the staff.

Centralized structure
An organization with a centralized organization structure has a strict chain of command, many management layers, and limited decision making authority. In a centralized structure, line and staff employees must get approvals from management before carrying out any business activity; all authority comes from upper or senior management. A centralized structure is characterized by a top-down management style. In a top-down style, all management decisions are made by upper management and these decisions are communicated to middle managers. The middle managers inform lower level managers or supervisors how to implement the decisions and the supervisors instruct staff members on what work needs to be done and how to perform the work.

Bureaucracy

A bureaucracy is an administrative structure used by large organizations. A bureaucracy is characterized by a hierarchical decision making and authority structure, highly defined areas of responsibility, promotions based on competence, and a fixed salary and wage structure. In a bureaucracy, there are many levels of tasks, responsibilities, and authority. These levels are delegated to any number of individuals or departments. To maintain cohesion, the organization is controlled by a central administration which oversees the entire operations of the organization. This central administration does not create products or provide services. Its purpose is to control, coordinate, and oversee the production and distribution of the products and services output by the organization. The goal of bureaucracy is to create efficiencies in large organizations. One of the disadvantages of a bureaucracy is that it is impersonal and employee needs and accomplishments are not recognized.

Departmentalization

Departmentalization is a structure where an organization is divided into functional responsibilities or areas. The division may be made by department or unit and the employees that specialize in a specific area are contained within that area. Examples of departments or units may be accounting, sales, marketing, research, and administration. There are five categories of departmentalization – product, geographic, customer, function, and process. When departmentalization is based on a product, a department is responsible for the product manufactured or service provided. Geographic departmentalization segregates departments based on the physical location of an organization's offices, retail outlets, or facilities. Departmentalization based on customers assigns departments based on the type of customer. Functional departmentalization defines departments based on an area of specialty. Process departmentalization assigns a step or steps in the production process to a department.

Task specialization

Task specialization occurs when an organization separates a process or job into a series of individual tasks. For each task, an individual employee or group of employees are assigned to complete only a single task. These employees are specialized at performing the assigned task and do not usually know how to perform other tasks within the process or job. In order for specialization to be efficient and productive, the organization needs to understand the limits of each employee's abilities and there must be no overlap between tasks. Each task must be completely separate from all other tasks. A disadvantage of task specialization is that employees are only trained to perform a specific task and the employees cannot easily move from one job function to another job function within the organization.

Division of labor

Division of labor occurs when an organization divides the labor force according to the work required to produce a product. This division is usually based on the task to be performed in the manufacturing process. Division of labor is seen in large manufacturing organizations that use mass production methods where each worker is specialized at performing one task. Smaller organizations do not benefit from division of labor. Smaller organizations do not have a large enough labor base that will allow each employee to perform one specific and specialized task. By using division of labor, an organization hopes to realize significant increases in productivity and reductions in costs. The disadvantage of division of labor is the possibility of conflicts and communication failure between specialized units. In addition, when employees perform a single specialized task, the organization takes the risk that employees will become bored or will suffer burnout because of the repetitive nature of their jobs.

Functions of management

Management is the process used to help an organization achieve its goals. To achieve these goals, management performs four functions within an organization – planning, organizing, directing, and controlling. Planning is the process of setting organizational goals and developing strategies that help the organization achieve these goals. Planning can include strategic planning, tactical planning, or contingency planning. Organizing is the process of allocating resources and assigning tasks in order to implement the strategies of the organization. When organizing, management develops processes in which employees, tasks, and resources are used efficiently and productively. Directing is the process of supervising the organization's employees in such a way as to accomplish the goals of the organization. Directing includes delegating tasks, assisting and training employees, adhering to the organization's policies, and evaluating employees. Controlling is the process of evaluating the performance of the organization's management. Controlling also includes correcting problems and keeping the organization within its goals.

Span of control

Span of control refers to the number of employees that a manager can supervise efficiently and effectively. Span of control may be limited due to the job or jobs performed by the employees, the skill and experience level of the employees, and the location of the employees. This limitation is the result of time constraints, energy levels, and attention to the job. When a manager operates outside their span of control, the growth of the organization is limited, the managers are less effective at dealing with employees, long-term plans and goals do not receive proper attention, and the organization may lose its competitive position. In addition, a manager who exceeds their span of control runs the risk of creating poor morale among subordinates, making poor or improper decision, and losing their entrepreneurial edge.

Reengineering

Reengineering is a means of reducing costs while increasing productivity and providing a higher level of service. It does this by changing the organization in the areas of employee hiring, technology, and business processes. Reengineering is usually attempted when an organization has failed in its other attempts to make changes and improvements. Reengineering is employed when serious measures need to be taken to facilitate change. When an organization decides to reengineer, it must first identify the problem and then determine how to fix the problem. Next, a reengineering model is developed and then the processes can be redesigned. Many reengineering projects fail because of a faulty design or lack of support from management and employees.

Reengineering uses technology and management to make systems, processes, and products more efficient, effective, and responsive. Efficiency, effectiveness, and responsiveness are measured in terms of the value provided to the customer. The goal of reengineering is to create a drastic improvement that will improve the quality of the product or service provided to the customer and to supply the product or service in the least amount of time possible. This is accomplished by making the organization more competitive, by reducing the amount of management needed to run the organization, and by providing more skilled labor. Reengineering is accomplished in three stages – definition, development, and deployment. When a process is reengineered, the process is examined, studied, and then modified in order to create a new process that retains the purpose of the reengineered process. A process may be reengineered to keep up with changes in the organization or in technology. The goal of process reengineering is to improve performance and to reduce costs.

Outsourcing

Outsourcing occurs when an organization procures the services of another organization in order to reduce costs and supply needed skills on a temporary basis. Outsourcing is seen in information technology when an organization needs to develop a new software application. The organization will hire a firm that specializes in software development. Another example is an organization that hires an independent accounting firm to perform its bookkeeping and recordkeeping functions instead of maintaining an internal accounting department. In these instances, it is more cost effective for the organization to purchase the product or service from an outside source than to spend the resources to produce the product or service internally. The downside of outsourcing is that the organization cannot maintain complete control over the quality and quantity of product or service it has purchased. The organization also has to include the cost of procuring the bids in the price of the outsourced product or service.

Strategic partnering

A strategic partnership is a legal contract between two organizations that have assets or skills that are beneficial to each other. An example would be a small, start-up firm that has a new idea for a product but does not have the capital or manufacturing facilities to develop the product. The small firm would partner with a larger firm that has the manufacturing facilities but not the technical knowledge of the smaller firm. Another example would be a manufacturer partnering with a wholesale distributor to share advertising and product development resources. This type of strategic partnering is found in the automobile and music industries. Strategic partnerships can cause problems when there is a dispute over intellectual property rights and the two firms cannot agree on the owner of an invention or technology. Problems also arise when the two firms become competitive with each other, when employees are hired away from one firm by the other, and when there is a disagreement as to the distribution of profits.

Lean thinking

Lean thinking is a technique used to produce a product so that the fewest resources are used. The goals are to reduce waste, improve quality, reduce production time, create a smooth process flow, cut costs, and improve customer value and satisfaction. There are a number of ways in which lean thinking is implemented. Products are produced in response to customer demand. Problems are identified and solved when and where they occur and the organization strives for zero defects. Activities that do not add value or are not a safety issue are minimized or eliminated so that scarce resources are used to their fullest capacity. The organization undertakes a process of continuous quality improvement to reduce costs, improve quality, and increase productivity. The organization strives to produce a mix of diverse products. Long term relationships are built with suppliers that include risk sharing, cost sharing, and information sharing. Production is kept at a constant level to keep waste at a minimum. And, the amount of work completed must be equal to the production plan.

Merger vs. acquisition

A business combination is called a *merger* when two (or, infrequently, more than two) companies are combined to form a single, new company. In this arrangement, often called a merger of equals, the shareholders of each of the merging companies exchange their holdings for a new issue of stock in a new company based upon an exchange ratio determined as part of the valuation process. A business combination where a company purchases the outstanding shares of another company is called an acquisition. The acquiring company exchanges cash or stock, or some combination thereof, for the shares of the target company. The acquiring company survives; the target company is dissolved. The expected benefit of such a combination is the expectation of synergy. That is, the whole (the new company) will be greater than the sum of the parts (the separate companies) reflected in cost reductions and other economies of scale, access to new markets and customers, improved access to capital, proprietary expertise, and technology.

Horizontal, vertical, conglomeration, purchase, and consolidation mergers

A horizontal merger is said to occur when both companies are competitors offering similar products and services in the same industry. The combination of two automobile manufacturers would be considered a horizontal merger. A vertical merger is said to occur when the two companies operate within the same or similar industry but at different levels.

The combination of a parts supplier and an automobile manufacturer would be considered a vertical merger. A conglomeration is said to occur when two companies with unrelated businesses are combined. The combination of an automobile manufacturer with an apparel maker would be considered a conglomeration. A purchase merger (or acquisition) is one in which some combination of cash and debt is exchanged for the outstanding shares of the target company. A consolidation merger is one in which only stock is used as the medium of exchange.

Reverse merger
A reverse merger is an alternative to an initial public offering (IPO) available to a private company. In such a transaction, the company acquires or otherwise merges with an existing shell company (an entity that has sold its assets and the encumbrance of its liabilities). The combined entity becomes a public company and can issue additional shares of stock.

Acquisitions
While it is common for an acquiring company to purchase the outstanding shares of a target company, it is also common for a company to purchase only the assets or the assets subject to the liabilities of the target company. In this case, the shell of the target company will survive the transaction, holding as its primary asset the consideration received. Shell companies will either liquidate, returning the net proceeds of the purchases to the shareholders, or restructure to enter another line of business.

Valuation methods for purchase price of target company

Three types of common valuation methods and the basis used for the determination of value are assets, income, or markets.
- Assets—A valuation method based upon assets sets the value of the acquisition based solely upon the value of the assets, exclusive of any encumbrances, using either the asset liquidation value or asset replacement cost as the key measure.
- Income—The income approach uses discounted cash flow analysis to determine the present value of the future income stream using an appropriate discount rate.
- Market—The market approach uses comparable companies with publicly available information as the basis for establishing value. For example, the value of the company may be measured using the same earnings multiple (price / earnings ratio) of a comparable company.

Divestiture

A divestiture is the opposite of an acquisition (just as divestment is the opposite of investment), whereby a company separates a portion of itself (such as a division or subsidiary) in a form of restructuring. Companies that initiate a divestiture typically seek to remove a business line that is unrelated to its core operations or is simply a poor fit requiring inordinate management attention. A subsidiary that operates in an aging business with modest growth prospects may be sold or spun off in order to focus on more promising opportunities. Alternatively, the divestment may be required by a regulatory authority, such as in compliance with an antitrust adjudication. Three of the common forms of divestiture include the following:
- Sell-off—In this form, a company sells the net assets of a division or the stock of a subsidiary outright in exchange for some form of consideration. The selling company relinquishes all ownership interest in the divested entity.

- Spin-off—A company that distributes assets to existing shareholders in the form of the stock of a new company is said to have created a spin-off. The existing shareholders thus become the new owners of the divested entity.
- Equity Carve-Out—In this form, a company engages in a sell-off but retains some portion of ownership or control of the removed entity, either by retaining some portion of existing stock or reserving a portion of a new public offering.

Risks

If the combination of entities seeks to achieve synergy, the divestiture of an entity would have the opposite effect. Where costs were reduced in combination by eliminating redundancies, improving efficiencies, and enjoying other benefits from economies of scale, divestiture creates the opposite effect. For example, the burden of sharing common administration, overhead, research and development, and other costs must be shared by fewer remaining entities. Also, the divested unit takes with it a talent pool and customer base that will no longer be available to the parent. The success of the divested unit is also not without risk. As a smaller entity without the support of a large parent, capital costs may increase, and some forms of capital may no longer be available. As a result, funding growth initiatives may become more difficult. The costs of operation may also be higher as services previously provided by the parent would need to be replaced.

Bankruptcy and bankruptcy discharge

Bankruptcy is the federal process established by the Bankruptcy Code of 1978, which as its objective, seeks to provide to debtors relief from unmanageable and burdensome debts. In this process, a judge of the federal bankruptcy court is empowered to administer the assets of the debtor in order to provide remuneration to the creditors (and consequent relief to the debtor). The bankruptcy discharge is the process whereby a debtor is relieved of liability for certain debts and creditors are prohibited from acting against the debtor in order to initiate collection.

Types

The three primary types of bankruptcy filing are as follows:
- Chapter 7—A filing under Chapter 7 (either by an individual or a commercial entity) seeks an orderly liquidation of the estate of a debtor. A trustee appointed by the court assumes control of the assets, converts the assets to cash, and distributes the proceeds to the creditors based upon various seniority rights.
- Chapter 11—A filing under Chapter 11 (by a commercial entity) seeks an orderly reorganization of the debts of the company with the goal of continuing business operations. The court will approve a plan of reorganization submitted either by the debtor or the creditors (by committee) or impose a plan of the court. A portion of the existing obligations of the debtor is repaid, and others are discharged.
- Chapter 13—A filing under Chapter 13 is essentially the equivalent of Chapter 11 but for a debtor that is an individual, the objective remaining partial repayment and discharge.

Prepackaged bankruptcy process

A bankruptcy process in which the plan of reorganization and repayment is negotiated and approved by all stakeholders (debtor, creditors, and stockholders) prior to the actual filing is said to be prepackaged. Such a process is more expedient than a traditional filing and typically incurs lower costs. Companies are able to file and emerge in a much shorter time frame.

<u>Absolute priority</u>
The rule of absolute priority establishes the order of payment to creditors and shareholders in a Chapter 11 filing. The first priority is granted to all creditors, while shareholders receive only any residual amounts. Within the creditor class, senior holders are compensated first followed by junior holders.

<u>Accounting challenges and requirements with Chapter 11 bankruptcy</u>
A company that enters into a Chapter 11 bankruptcy filing is first required to record all transactions originating from bankruptcy events separate from those of continuing operations. That is, pre-petition accounts must be separated from post-petition accounts. In addition, the income and expenses associated with the bankruptcy filing are required to be reported as reorganization items in the financial statements. Once a reorganization plan has been approved, the effect on liabilities from partial payments and discharges must be determined, often resulting in valuation issues. The reduction in value is called compromise, and the affected liabilities must be segregated from post-petition items. Once a company emerges from a Chapter 11 proceeding, it may be subject to fresh start accounting methodology if certain asset and shareholder equity values are present. Such methodology can be complex as it seeks to revalue the balance sheet on a pro forma basis.

Foreign exchange

Foreign exchange is the exchange of currencies between governments and businesses of different nations. This currency is used to settle trade between nations. Foreign exchange converts the money of one nation into the money of another nation in order to pay the debts of the first nation. Trading in foreign currencies sets the value for products and resources imported and exported between nations. This trade is done on an over-the-counter market. This over-the-counter market is a network of banks, brokers, and individuals who exchange currencies over an electronic network. Trading does not take place in a physical financial market.

Current account

The current account is the sum of a nation's net revenue from import and export trade, tourism income, overseas profits, and interest payments from foreign nations. Net revenues from import and export trade are normally the largest component of the current account. When exports are higher than imports, there is usually a current account surplus. When imports are greater than exports, there is usually a current account deficit. Because exports generate positive net sales, and because the trade balance is typically the largest component of the current account, a current account surplus is usually associated with positive net exports.

Balance of payments

Balance of payments is the record of a nation's payments to, and receipts from, foreign nations. The payments also including the price of imports, the outflow of capital, and the outflow of gold. The receipts also include the price of exports, the inflow of capital, and the inflow of gold. A negative or deficit balance of payments means imports are greater than exports and that more money is flowing out of the nation. A positive or surplus balance of payments means that exports are greater than imports and the more money is flowing into the nation. Balance of payments is used as an indicator of a nation's economic and political stability. Balance of payments is divided into two categories: the Current Account and the Capital Account.

Official reserve account

The official reserve account is an accounting of a nation's reserves. Reserves include official gold reserves, foreign exchange reserves, and IMF Special Drawing Rights. Reserve accounts typically are dominated by monetary authority intervention in the official currency's exchange rate. Nations use the official reserve account to control the price of their currency. The more control a nation tries to exert over its currency, the larger the fluctuation in their official reserve account. An increase in the official reserve account means that a nation is buying its currency to keep the price high. A decrease in the official reserve account means that a nation wants to keep the price of its currency low.

Capital account

The capital account is also known as the financial account. It is a measure of investment in a nation made by foreign investors. It is the sum of a nation's bank deposits, investments by private investors, and debt securities sold by a central bank or a government agency. The financial account shows change in foreign ownership of domestic assets. If foreign ownership of domestic assets is greater than domestic ownership of foreign assets, there is a financial account surplus. If domestic ownership of foreign assets is greater than foreign ownership of domestic assets, there is a financial account deficit.

Effects of trade deficit and trade surplus

A trade deficit occurs when there are more imported products coming into a nation than exported products leaving a nation. A trade surplus occurs when exports are greater than imports. A trade deficit or trade surpluses determine a nation's balance of trade. Balance of trade is affected by the strength of a nation's currency against the currency of other nations, a nation's manufacturing advantage over foreign nations, and the state of a nation's economy. When there is a trade deficit, a nation is losing capital which can cause interest rates to increase.

Exchange rate

The exchange rate is the price of one nation's currency when converted into another nation's currency. It is the rate that one currency can be converted into another currency. A number of factors determine the exchange rate for different currencies. Some exchange rates are determined by trading activity in the currency market. Some exchange rates are determined by agreement. The spot exchange rate is the current exchange rate. The forward exchange rate is an exchange rate that is quoted and traded today but delivery and payment is at a future date.

Fixed exchange rate
A fixed exchange rate is an exchange rate that is agreed upon by two nations. A fixed exchange rate is regulated by monetary policy. The gold standard is the most well known

fixed exchange rate system. The purpose of a fixed exchange rate system is to maintain a nation's currency value within a very narrow margin. Under a fixed exchange rate system, a nation is required to maintain its currency at or near the fixed rate. Fixed exchange rates were established in 1944 at the Bretton Woods International Monetary Conference. Fixed exchange rates were used until the 1970s. When the United States abandoned the gold standard, a flexible or floating exchange rate system was adopted. Fixed exchange rates are maintained in the same way interest rates are maintained. The rate is kept stable by the use of open market operations when a currency is sold to the market, or purchased from the market. This buying and selling of a currency is done by a central monetary authority. The only difference between regulating currency prices and interest rates is the target of the intervention. Most monetary authorities use their authority to target interest rates rather than exchange rates.

Advantages and disadvantages: Fixed exchange rates are not linked and do not respond to the foreign exchange markets. This means that a currency is not priced at its true market value. Fixed exchange rates do not give nations the ability to achieve an independent domestic monetary policy which can lead to internal stability. Even though a fixed exchange rate system does not give a nation the power to compete with other currencies, it may give a nation greater economic stability.

Quotes
Exchange rates are quoted as the number of units of a price currency that can be traded in terms of 1 unit currency. Quotes that use a nation's currency as the price currency are called direct quotation or price quotation. Quotes that use a nation's currency as the unit currency are called indirect quotation or quantity quotation. When a nation's currency is strengthening, the exchange rate goes down. When a foreign currency is strengthening, the exchange rate goes up, which depreciates a nation's currency.

Flexible or floating exchange rate
A flexible exchange rate occurs when two nations agree to let international market forces set the exchange rate. A flexible exchange rate is determined by supply and demand of one currency relative to other currencies. It also fluctuates with a nation's exports and imports. Flexible exchange rates change constantly and are determined by trading in the foreign exchange market. In a flexible exchange rate system, the exchange rate changes when the values of the traded currencies change. A currency becomes more valuable when the demand is greater than the supply. It becomes less valuable when demand is less than supply. This may be because individuals prefer holding their wealth in some other form. An increase in currency demand may be due to either an increased transaction demand for money or an increased speculative demand for money. The transaction demand for money is correlated to the country's level of business activity, gross domestic product, and employment. The speculative demand for money is tied to interest rates. The higher a nation's interest rates, the greater the demand for its currency. In addition, currency loses value if the nation's inflation rate is high, if output is expected to decline, or if there is political uncertainty.

Advantages and disadvantages: In a flexible exchange rate system, a central bank needs to become involved in the buying and selling of currency to keep exchange rates from becoming too high or too low. This intervention may be minimal if the goal is to only maintain market stability. If the goal is to keep a currency within a desired range, a greater amount of intervention will be needed. A fixed exchange rate system has the advantage of lessening the effects of financial downturns and business cycles.

Factors that determine currency rates: In a flexible exchange rate system, the value of currency is determined by the supply of and demand for a currency. The supply and demand of a currency depends on the current account balance for a nation, the strength of the nation's economy, the nation's inflation rate, and the nation's interest rate compared to other nations.

International Monetary Fund

The International Monetary Fund is an international organization was formed in 1944. Its purpose is to maintain monetary stability in the foreign exchange market. The IMF works with developing nations to manage their foreign debts. The role of the IMF is to monitor economic and financial developments, lend funds to nations that have balance of payment problems, and provide assistance and training. The purpose of the IMF is to promote monetary stability, facilitate the growth of international trade, and create a system for international payments.

World Bank

The World Bank is an international organization that offers financing, information, training, and research to developing nations. The World Bank is able to provide loans by selling bonds in the capital markets of member countries and from contributions of its members. It was originally formed at the end of World War II to help European and Asian nations with postwar reconstruction. The purpose of the World Bank today is to reduce poverty in middle income and poor income nations. Their goal is to help people help themselves.

Direct foreign investment

Direct foreign investment is when a nation invests in a foreign organization and also controls the foreign organization. A nation may invest in a foreign corporation when it is looking for resources, markets, or efficiency. Sometimes it is more economical for a nation to invest is foreign resources when those resources cost less or are more efficient to obtain in a foreign nation. A nation may look for new markets or maintain existing markets by investing in foreign organizations. Most nations will make a foreign investment to increase their efficiency by taking advantage of economies of scale.

Risks
The risks of direct foreign investment are political risk and exchange rate risk. Political risk is a financial risk that a nation's government will change its policies. These policy changes may have a significant effect on the financial instruments of the nation. Exchange rate risk is the risk that the value of an investment will change based on changes in currency exchange rates. Exchange rate risk affects organizations that import and export products and services.

American Depository Receipt

An American Depository Receipt is a receipt issued by an American bank to American investors instead of taking stock ownership in foreign organizations. American Depository

Receipts are traded on stock exchanges and over the counter markets. Stock dividends are paid to holders of American Depository Receipts in the form of cash or ADR dividends.

Trade financing methods

Letters of credit

Letters of credit are used to guarantee that a buyer will pay for products received from a seller. Letters of credit also act as insurance for the buyer by ensuring that they will receive the product. The bank states that it will pay the amount due if the purchaser does not make the agreed upon payment. In addition, the bank also makes sure that the products have been shipped before payment will be made to the seller.

Forfaiting

Forfaiting is the purchase of the amount importers owes an exporter. These accounts receivable are purchased at a discount by paying cash. The importers are no longer obligated to pay the exporter. The importers pay the forfaiater, the organization that purchased the obligations. In this arrangement, the exporter is paid for products sold and does not have the risk of not receiving payment from the importers.

Banker's acceptances

A banker's acceptance is a short term bill of exchange that is guaranteed by a bank. The bank guarantees that the issuer of the bill of exchange will pay the face value of the bill by the due date. If the issuer defaults on the bill, the bank pays the obligation. When a bank guarantees payment of a transaction in this manner, it makes it easier for organizations to conduct international trade.

Countertrade

Countertrade is a nation's trading of products that it produces for the products produced by another nation. Money is not used as a medium of exchange. The nation receiving the products may use the products or may sell them for cash.

Transfer pricing

Transfer pricing is the pricing and sale of products and services within a multinational organization. It is used in cross-border transactions. A multinational organization may sell products to a foreign subsidiary and set the sales price so that profits are allocated to different divisions based on the tax burden placed on each division in each nation. Transfer pricing occurs when one segment of an organization charges another segment within the organization for the products and services provided to that segment. There is a buyer and seller relationship between the two segments. Transfer pricing is used when each segment within the organization is a separate responsibility center. In a decentralized organization, a segment may sell a product to another product for the same price as it would sell the product to an outside customer. This motivates managers to work in the best interest of the organization. Transfer pricing is minimally concerned with equally and fairly distributing costs between segments. It is more concerned in creating goal congruence within the organization and providing factors for motivation. Transfer pricing is used mostly by investment and profit centers; whereas the costs of a cost center are distributed to the producing segments of an organization.

<u>Benefits</u>
Transfer pricing gives a segment within an organization to operate as a separate entity, to achieve the goals of the segment, and to operate in the best interests of the organization. Transfer pricing promotes goal congruence, increases managerial effort, and provides motivation. Transfer pricing allows segments to achieve their goals because they receive a fair price for products and services sold to other segments within the organization. In addition, those segments that use products and services pay a fair price for the product or service received. When a segment is compensated for those products and services provided to other segments, managers are more likely to continue working toward achieving the goals of an organization.

<u>Transfer pricing policy factors</u>
The choice of a transfer pricing policy depends on a number of factors. The transfer price for the product or service must promote the goals of the organization. The transfer price should be set so that the segment selling the product or service is able to recover its incremental cost plus the opportunity cost of the transfer. The opportunity cost is the profit the segment would have received if the product or service were sold to an outside buyer. Segments should be allowed to negotiate the transfer price. The purchasing segment should be able to purchase the product or service at the same price as it would pay if purchasing from an outside seller. Transfers should only be initiated if the segment supplying the product or service has the capacity to produce the product or service needed by the other segments within the organization. The ability of segments to transfer products and services between each other will depend on the tax liability placed on the organization for the transfers.

Decision Analysis

CVP analysis

Cost/volume/profit (CVP) analysis is a planning decision method that shows how costs and profits may change depending on the volume of output. It looks at factors such as variable costs, fixed costs, sales price, production volume, and product mix to determine the possible amount of change in costs and profits. CVP can help management decide on the sales volume needed to break even and the sales volume needed to earn a specific profit. It shows how changes in the sales price and costs affect profits. It also shows how a change in the product mix can affect the break even point and potential profits.

Fixed costs and variable costs

Variable costs are costs or expenses that vary depending on the level of production. This level of production is the number of units produced in a manufacturing environment. In a service environment, it may be the number of clients serviced. Variable costs include expenses such as materials and labor. Fixed costs are expenses that do not vary with different levels of production. These costs may include rent, insurance, and management salaries. Categories of expenses that can be considered both a fixed and a variable cost include utilities, insurance, and taxes. In these instances, a portion of the expenses need to be paid no matter what the level of production. For utilities, there is a base fee that is not dependent on the amount of the resource used. This is the fixed portion of the expense. The rest of the utilities expense is dependent on the amount of resource used and a fee is charged on a usage basis. In addition, some of the resource may still need to be used even during periods of no or low production activity.

Variable costs are used to determine the contribution margin. The contribution margin is the difference between the per-unit variable cost and the selling price per unit. The contribution margin determines the break even point. Variable costs determine the cost of goods sold. Cost of goods sold is one way that an organization can measure its productivity. Variable costs may or may not change as production volume changes. Variable costs will decline on a per unit basis as the quantity manufactured or sold increases if economies of scale can be realized, for example, by ordering larger quantities of raw materials. In contrast, fixed costs do change with the level of production. As production increases, the allocation of fixed costs per unit of production decreases.

Breakeven

Breakeven is the point where the investment that an organization makes in a product equals the return that the organization receives from the product. It is also the point in a product's growth cycle where its sales equal its costs. Sales that are above the breakeven point result in a profit. Sales below the breakeven point result in a loss.

Marginal analysis

Marginal analysis is a economic technique that measures incremental increases and decreases in an organization's operations. To aid in the decision making process it also uses the concepts of marginal revenue, marginal cost, and marginal profit. It measures the effects of changes when money, material, product, labor, or other factors fluctuate by one unit. It is used to determine how these changes affect an organization's market, production, and business cycle. Marginal analysis looks at all of these factors in order to obtain an optimal decision.

Contribution margin

Contribution margin is a method used by an organization to calculate the profitability of a single product. Contribution margin is the result of subtracting the variable costs attributed to a product from the total revenue received from that product. The contribution margin is used when an organization needs to decide whether to add a product or discontinue a product. It aids in determining the price at which to sell a product. It can also be used to set sales commissions and bonuses.

Opportunity cost

Opportunity cost is the cost of choosing one course of action over another course of action in the decision making process. This cost is the benefits that are not received from the action that was not chosen. For example, an organization may make a decision between marketing one of two products. The product that is not chosen for market has as its opportunity cost the income that will not be derived from the sales of that product. An organization will incur an opportunity cost when a decision is made not to take a particular course of action. The opportunity cost is the lost benefit or lost income of not taking the alternative course of action. For example, if an organization has money to invest it may have the opportunity to invest in new equipment or it may want to invest in income producing securities. If the organization invests in securities, the opportunity cost is the difference between the income produced by the securities and the predicted lost income from additional sales that could have been produced by the addition of new equipment and increased product production.

Disadvantages
One disadvantage of using opportunity cost when making a decision is that it is difficult to list all of the relevant costs. This is because an organization may not have enough information when making the decision and will overlook an aspect of an action. This oversight can result in significant costs being ignored. Another disadvantage is that costs that are relevant to the action being decided upon will not be included in the decision. Again, this may be due to a lack of information.

Make-or-buy decision

A make-or-buy decision compares the feasibility of producing a product in house against purchasing a product from another supplier. It would be feasible to manufacture a product if the cost to manufacture is lower than the cost to purchase the product. Another instance where it might be feasible to manufacture a product would be if the organization has excess capacity that needs to be utilized. An organization may elect to buy a product if it wishes to maintain alternative sources of supply, if it wants design flexibility, or if it desires to maintain access to innovative sources of supply.

<u>Qualitative and quantitative factors</u>
Qualitative factors that an organization needs to consider when deciding whether to make a product in house or to buy it from an outside supplier include product quality and maintaining relationships with suppliers. The organization must also decide whether to use existing facilities or leave them idle. Quantitative factors are those factors that deal with the cost of producing the product or the cost of buying the product.

Relevant costs and relevant revenues in decision making process

Relevant costs and relevant revenues occur in the future when the decision is implemented. If costs and revenues occurred in the past and are not going to occur in the future, these costs and revenues cannot be considered in the decision making process. Relevant costs and revenues must be different for each option being considered in the decision.

Avoidable and unavoidable costs

An avoidable cost is a cost that will not be incurred by an organization if they discontinue a product or do not pursue a course of action. All costs are considered avoidable except for sunk costs and costs that the organization will continue to incur regardless of whether the product or action is continued. For example, if an organization chooses to discontinue manufacturing a product, the labor and material costs associated with that product are avoidable costs. That is, when manufacturing of the product is suspended, the organization will no longer incur those costs. Avoidable costs are usually variable costs to the organization. Unavoidable costs are costs that will be incurred whether or not an organization decides to discontinue a product or course of action. Unavoidable costs are usually fixed costs.

Cost behavior patterns

A cost behavior pattern is how costs change according to the level of manufacturing activity. These costs may be variable, fixed, or a combination of the two. If the cost is a combination of fixed and variable, the cost needs to be itemized so that the fixed costs are separated from the variable costs. This breakdown can be accomplished by using either the High-Low Method or the Least-Squares Method.

Incremental costs

Incremental costs are also referred to as differential costs or relevant costs. These are the differences in costs when two or more alternative decision possibilities are being considered. Incremental costs can be calculated when there are changes in manufacturing output. The incremental cost is the difference between each level of output change.

Unavoidable cost

An unavoidable cost is a cost or expense that an organization will incur no matter what decision is made to continue or suspend a project or task. If an organization decides to discontinue manufacturing a product, the organization will still incur the costs of rent and utilities. The only way to avoid the rent expense would be to move out of the facility the organization used to manufacture the product. Unavoidable costs cannot be recovered or saved. Unavoidable costs are usually fixed costs to the organization.

Qualitative factors and quantitative factors

Qualitative factors are factors in the decision making process that cannot be measured in monetary terms. Qualitative factors do have intrinsic value. They may enhance or detract from situations that do have value to the organization. The situations may include employee morale, production schedules, supplier relationships, customer relationships, and future profitability. In many situations, qualitative factors are more important in the decision making process than actions that can be measured in monetary terms. Qualitative factors play an important role in the viability and long-term growth of an organization. They assure that the organization can run at a high level of production and can help ensure future profitability. Quantitative factors are those factors in the decision making process that are measured in terms of money.

Sunk costs

Sunk costs are costs that have been realized as part of a project and cannot be changed by any action taken or decision made by an organization. Sunk costs are usually expenditures that have taken place in the past and the amount spent cannot be recovered by the sale of the item purchased. Sometimes these items are considered obsolete or they have reached the end of their useful life. Sunk costs should not be considered when making a decision because these costs are historical and may not reflect the current value of the item being decided upon and are not an indication of replacement cost.

Target marketing

A company cannot compete in every market that might take an interest in its products or services. It is just not cost effective. Therefore, it is essential that the company select those market segments where their products and services have the highest chance of making the sale and of making a profit. Market segmentation occurs when the company breaks down a market according to the characteristics of the buyers in the larger market. Targeting occurs when the company selects those segments that contain the characteristics or traits which it can best service. Usually, a company will select those segments that either contain the largest number of consumers, offer the best opportunities, or have been neglected by the competition. Positioning occurs when the company begins to advertise and take other actions so that the consumer becomes aware of what the company has to offer in the form of products and services.

Segmented industrial markets

Industrial markets are segmented according to the type of organization, how they operate their business, and their purchase practices. Organizational segments include business type and business size. Operational segments include products manufactured, manufacturing processes, and amount of product produced. Purchase practices segments include a business' purchasing policies, vendor relationships, product quality, and product availability.

Market segmentation

Market segmentation is a method to first group potential customers according to common needs and then to group them according to buying behavior. In this way, each individual segment can be determined to respond in the same way to a marketing technique. In market segmentation, customers are grouped in several ways. A segment can be based on demographic information such as age, race, income, education, and occupation. Segments can be based on psychographic information such as attitudes, lifestyle, hobbies, and political views. Segments can be based on where people live or their geographic area. This can be a city, a neighborhood, an urban area, a rural area. Or it may be based on population base or the climate and weather. When customers have a predetermined benefit that they want to receive from a product, this market may be segmented according to product-benefit. These benefits may be quality, performance, features, or price.

Market segmentation is not an easy strategy to pursue when selecting markets for products and services. The consumers that belong to a market segment must be identified in terms of having a shared characteristic and that characteristic must be measurable. The process of dividing a market into segments can be costly. Therefore, the segment must be large enough to generate enough sales volume to cover marketing and manufacturing costs in order to be profitable. The market segment must be reachable so that the company can gain the attention of the segment. The segment must be responsive to the product or service and willing to make a purchase. The consumers in a segment and their characteristic must not change over the short term; the segment must be stable in their wants and needs.

Positioning strategies

The goal of a good marketer is to guide a consumer's behavior by helping the consumer come to a specific conclusion about the product or service. The most common positioning strategy is to associate a product with one or more specific features or characteristics. Positioning can also be accomplished by focusing on the benefits, needs, and solutions a product addresses. These two positioning strategies give the consumer a reason for buying the product. Advantages can be gained by giving the product the perception of being high in quality. The higher price of high quality can be justified by adding additional services or features to the product giving the consumer the perceived notion that they will gain from these additions. Positioning can be attained by giving the product a specific use or by associating the product with a well-known celebrity. Another way to position a product is to take a stand in relation to a competing company or product. This is done by using comparative advertising.

Supply and demand

Price of products and services
When a producer puts a product or service on the market, they base the sales price on past experience. They set a price which they feel the consumers will pay and produce a quantity that will sell. If the producer sells more product at that price, the price will rise because as demand increases so does the price. In addition, more products will be supplied to the market because as prices increase the producer will want to sell more products. If, on the other hand, the supply of the product is larger than the demand, the price of the product will decrease. This decrease in price will create a demand from people who were unwilling to buy at the higher price.

<u>Supply and demand graph</u>
A supply and demand graph is made up of two curves. The demand curve slopes downward to the right and shows that as prices decline, the quantity demanded increases. The supply curve slopes upward to the right. It shows that as the prices increases, producers supply more products and services. The point at which these two curves intersect is the equilibrium price. The equilibrium price is the price at which producers supply the same quantity of a product as the consumers will use.

<u>Law of demand</u>
Demand is the quantity of products or services that is desired by buyers. This quantity is determined by the amount of product or service that buyers will purchase at a certain price. The amount that buyers will purchase will vary given different prices for the product or service. When all factors of a product or service except price are equal, the higher the price of the product or service, the less the buyers will demand the product or service. This is because at higher prices, buyers are less willing to give up other products and services that they need. The lower the price, the higher the quantity demanded.

<u>Law of supply</u>
Supply is the quantity of products or services that the market has available for sale. This quantity is determined by the price that can be received for the product or service. The amount of products and services that will be supplied will vary given different prices for the product or service. The higher the price, the higher the quantity supplied. This is because at higher prices a producer will receive a higher revenue.

Effect of surplus on price

A surplus occurs when too much product is being produced and too little product is being consumed. When there is a surplus of a product on the market, this means that the price has been set too high. The quantity produced is higher than the quantity demanded. Producers set this higher price to create more revenue and increase their profits. The producer can either keep this higher price in the hope that the higher price will result in a reasonable profit. Or, the producer can lower the price to sell off their surplus quantity of product.

Market equilibrium price

The market equilibrium price is when the amount of product or services supplied equals the amount of product or services demanded. At this price, the allocation of products or services is at its most efficient point. Efficiency occurs when the amount being supplied exactly equals the amount being demanded. This is the optimum economic situation because producers are selling all of their product and consumers are getting all the product they need and want. This equilibrium price is only a theory. The prices of products and services constantly change in relation to fluctuations in demand and supply.

Product pricing strategies

Competition based pricing is used when an organization sets the price of their product based on the price of competing products. Cost-plus pricing uses the cost to produce a product as the base and then adds a percentage to the cost to come up with a selling price. Skimming is when a product is sold at a high price to gain a high profit. Skimming helps an organization recoup its investment in research and development of the product. Limit pricing decreases the ability of competitors to enter a market and to take advantage of the lower costs of economies of scale. Loss leader is used to attract customers to buy other products sold by the organization. Penetration pricing allows a product to quickly enter a market by selling at a lower price.

Competition-based pricing and cost-based pricing
Competition-based pricing uses competitors' prices to set the price for a product. This is used when there is very little or no difference between an organization's product and the competitor's product. This makes it easier to compete in the market but does not take into account the cost to manufacture the product. Cost-based pricing uses the cost to manufacture the product as the base and then adds a percentage. This percentage equates to the product's profit margin. This method does not take into consideration the demand for the product or what the customers are willing to pay for the product.

Market skimming pricing and market penetration pricing
Pricing strategies are used by an organization to achieve its goals and to earn a profit. Penetration pricing is used when an organization wants to increase its market share in a short period of time and to generate repeat sales. To do this, an organization needs to build customer loyalty quickly. This can be done by giving out free samples or offering discounts to new customers. Price skimming is done when an organization sells a small amount of its product at a high price in the beginning and then begins to lower the price at a later time. In the beginning, the organization realizes the highest profit margin. This enables to organization to recover high development costs. Then, later, the organization realizes higher sales volume. Using this approach, an organization can reach a larger market share.

Effect of shortage on price

A shortage occurs when there is not enough of a product being produced to satisfy the wants of the consumers. When there is not enough products to supply the market, this means that the price has been set too low. The quantity produced is lower than the quantity demanded. Because of consumer competition for the product, the producers can raise their prices. This increase in price gives producers an incentive to produce more products to increase supply. This price increase can only continue until the amount being supplied meets the amount being demanded.

Price-adjustment strategies

Discount and allowances pricing offers incentives to customers to buy a product. These incentives may include cash or seasonal discounts, and trade-in and promotional allowances. Segmented pricing is when a product or service is sold at different prices depending on different segment characteristics. Psychological pricing uses motivation factors, such as the relationship between price and quality, to encourage a customer to purchase a product. Promotional pricing is when a product is temporarily reduced in price to help increase sales in the short-term. Geographical and international pricing may price products at different prices depending on where the customer is located and the demand for the product.

Making pricing decisions

The price an organization should charge for its products depends on a number of factors. The organization needs to consider how much the competition charges for a similar product, how much it costs for the organization to produce the product, how much advertising is needed to get the product to market, and what promotion methods will need to be used to create customer interest. Most organizations initially price a product using a cost-plus pricing method. Once the product has a sales history, the price may be adjusted according to market conditions and competing products on the market.

Cost-based pricing

Cost-based pricing uses either variable costs or full costs as the basis of setting a price for a product. The disadvantages of using this method are that there may not be any incentive to control costs and that it focuses on controlling costs rather than maximizing profits. The advantages are that it may result in the most advantageous utilization of the organization's resources and thereby increase profits.

Target cost

The target cost is the difference between the target price of a product and the expected profit. The target cost is used as a basis for developing a product that can be designed and manufactured at the price at or below this target cost. The target cost is the maximum cost that the organization desires to pay to produce a product. The target cost includes the production and operating costs. If the actual cost of producing a product exceeds the target cost, the organization may find it is no longer profitable to manufacture a product. It is not always feasible to increase the target price in order to cover the costs above the target cost. The customer may not be willing to pay the additional price. A target cost is an expense incurred in the production of a product, or the cost of operations of the organization to reach the level of service that should be attained. Performance is determined by comparing the target cost to the actual cost. If there is a difference between the two, it is called a variance. These variances may indicate that there are inefficiencies in the production process and corrective action may need to be taken.

Target pricing

Target pricing is a method of setting a selling price for a product so that a specific rate of return for a level of production is achieved. Target pricing is used by organizations that have a large capital investment in their manufacturing facilities. Examples include utility companies, airplane manufacturers, and automobile manufacturers. Target pricing is not used by organizations that have a low capital investment because it will result in a lower than profitable sales price for their product. In addition, target pricing is not linked to demand for a product. If the entire product inventory is not sold, the organization will incur a loss. Before a target price can be set, the organization must first determine the price at which the product will be competitive with similar products in the market and the profit which it wants to make from the product. Then, a target price is set based on what the organization believes the customer will pay for the product. To set a target price, the organization relies on market research and by determining the costs involved in getting the product to the customer. Sometimes, the target price is based according to the sales prices of similar products on the market.

The target price of a product should be reviewed when market conditions change. These market conditions may include inflation and cost of living increases. Inflation can increase the target cost because of increases in fuel, transportation, material, and labor costs. These cost increases mean that the organization will need to increase the sales price of the product to maintain profitability. Cost of living increases will reduce the ability of the customer to pay a higher price for a product. To overcome these obstacles, an organization may want to use marketing techniques such as redesigning, resizing, repackaging, and reviving of the product.

Value engineering

Value engineering is a method used to attain the minimum target cost without decreasing the level of customer satisfaction. It looks at all of the elements of the product such as research and development, design, production, marketing, distribution, and customer service. The goal is to control costs at the design stage of product development when the costs are incurred. After the design stage, costs are locked in and cannot be changed as a result of the decisions made. Locked in costs are the result of resources that have been used in the manufacturing process.

Target operating income per unit and target cost per unit

The target operating income per unit is the income that an organization predicts it can earn on each unit of a product sold. The target cost per unit is the cost that an organization estimates it will pay to produce each unit of product. The target cost per unit enables an organization to meet its target operating income per unit goal when selling the product at the target price. The target cost per unit is calculated by subtracting the target operating income per unit from the target price.

Value-added cost and nonvalue-added cost

A value-added cost is a cost that adds to the actual or perceived value of a product or service. A value-added cost raises the value of the product which in turn may mean increased income to the organization. A nonvalue-added cost does not add to or detract from a product's perceived value or usefulness to a customer. A nonvalue-added cost does affect an organization's profitability but does not have an effect on the sales of a product.

Elasticity

Elasticity is the degree to which a demand or supply curve reacts to a change in the price of a product or service. Elasticity is the percentage change in quantity divided by the percentage change in price. If elasticity is greater than or equal to one, the curve is elastic. If it is less than one, the curve is inelastic. Not all products have the same degree of elasticity. The demand for products that consumers need no matter what the price tends to be less affected by price changes. Consumers will purchase the product no matter what the price. The demands for products that are not essential to consumers are more affected by price changes. When the price for these products goes up, the demand will go down.

Price elasticity of demand

Price elasticity of demand is a measure of consumer behavior that shows that the quantity of a product or service that the consumers demand depends on the increase or decrease in the price of the product or service. It is the percent change in the quantity demanded divided by the percent change in price. Price elasticity of demand is determined by several factors. These factors include the price of the product or service, the availability of alternative products, the time period involved, consumer income, and whether the product is a necessity or a luxury.

There are three factors that affect the price elasticity of demand. The first is the availability of substitutes. When consumers have other products from which to choose, the demand will be elastic. When there are no substitutes, the product will have an inelastic demand. A product is elastic when an increase in the price causes a decrease in demand because consumers will buy another product that meets their needs. The second factor is the amount of income that the consumer has available to spend on the product. When the price of a product goes up and the consumer does not have the additional money to spend on the product, the demand is elastic and demand will go down. The last factor is time. If the price of a product that the consumer needs goes up and the consumer cannot afford the increased price, the consumer will begin to reduce their need for the product. In this case, the price elasticity becomes elastic over the long term.

When the price elasticity of demand is greater than 1, the percentage change in quantity is greater than the change in price. This means that the demand for the product is considered elastic and an increase in price reduces the revenues for the product. When the price elasticity of demand is less than 1, percentage change in quantity is smaller than that in price. This means that the demand for the product is considered inelastic and an increase in price increases revenues for the product. When the price elasticity of demand is equal to 1, percentage change in quantity is equal to the change in price. This means that the demand is unitary elastic and an increase in price does not change revenue. When the price elasticity of demand is equal to 0, changes in price do not affect the quantity demanded for the product.

Inelastic demand

On the demand curve, inelastic demand is represented by an upright curve. This upright curve shows that a price increase does not necessarily create an increase or decrease in the quantity demanded. As prices go up, so do total revenues. In addition, costs do not increase and may be reduced which will result in an increase in profit.

Elastic demand

On the demand curve, elastic demand is represented by a flatter curve. This flat curve shows that a small increase in price causes a large decrease in quantity demanded. Or, a decrease in price causes an increase in quantity demanded.

Price elasticity of supply

The price elasticity of supply is a measure of how a change in price affects the quantity of a product that producers are willing to supply. The price elasticity of supply is the percentage change in supply divided by the percentage change in price. When this figure is more than 1, the supply is elastic. When this figure is less than 1, the supply is inelastic. When the supply is elastic, a change in price will increase the amount of a product that is supplied.

Income elasticity of demand

Income elasticity of demand measure how much a change in consumers' income changes the quantity of a product or service that the consumers demand. The amount of this change depends on whether the product or service is a necessity or a luxury. When income increases, so does the demand for products and services. But, the demand for necessities increases at a slower rate than the increase in income. During these periods of increased income, consumers are more likely to increase their spending on luxury products.

Cross elasticity of demand

Cross elasticity of demand is a measure of how the quantity of a product or service demanded responds to the change in the price of another product or service. Cross elasticity of demand is the percentage change in demand for one product divided by the percentage change in price to a second product. When the two products are complements (that is, one is used in conjunction with the other), an increase in the price of one will cause a decrease in the demand of the other. When two products are substitutes for each other, an increase in price of one will cause an increase in the demand for the other.

Product life cycle

There are four stages in the life cycle of a product. The first is the introductory stage where the product shows slow growth in the market and obtains a low profit margin. At this stage, customers are unfamiliar with the product and may be hesitant to use the product. If the product does gain acceptance with the customers, it goes into a growth stage. At this stage, the product moves into new markets because of improved distribution channels. At the end of the growth cycle is the maturity stage. At this point, sales of the product, along with its profits, begin to stabilize. As consumers lose interest in the product, it goes into a decline stage where sales and profits begin to decrease.

Target rate of return pricing

Target rate of return pricing is used by monopolies to achieve a specified return on invested capital. The organization first starts with the rate of return that it wants to realize from the sale of its product. Then it sets the price based on the cost to produce the product and adding the rate of return. The goal is to keep the target rate of return at a constant level. This is done by changing the price of the product as demand for the product changes.

Peak-load pricing

Peak-load pricing is a method of increasing the price of a product when the demand for the product is at its highest level. This method works well for organizations when they need to recoup a major portion of their investment in the development of a product. It is most often used by utility companies who have made a substantial investment to make sure that their customers have access to services even when demand for the service is at its highest point.

This type of investment is usually made when the demand for the service has reached the physical limit of the utility company to provide the service.

Life-cycle costing

Life-cycle costing is a method of reducing the costs involved with manufacturing a product during the different stages in the product's life cycle. It also attempts to lengthen the product's life span. To reduce costs, an organization needs to look at such ratios as net present value, internal rate of return, and discounted cash flow in order to reduce future costs of the product. Costs that can be reduced include machinery maintenance, labor and salaries, and transportation.

Risk Management

Risk and risk management framework

Risk in general can be defined as the effect of uncertainty due to a deficiency of information with respect to events. For example, the effect of not knowing when the next earthquake will occur creates risk of harm and loss for individuals and entities within an affected area. Risk management refers to a structured process consisting of plans and actions intended to mitigate the effects of risk. The risk of damage from an earthquake is mitigated by retrofitting buildings, automatic utility shutdown, shatterproof glass, duck-and-cover plans, evacuation plans, emergency medical assistance availability, and so on. A risk management framework is a structure that supports the risk management process by providing for foundational support (policies, procedures, and the commitment of management to execute) and organizational support (accountability structure, plans, resources, and activities).

Risk assessment process

The process of risk assessment consists of three components:
- Risk identification—The identification of risks involves applying historical data, employing professional advisors, conducting analytical studies, and other actions in order to determine potential risk factors.
- Risk analysis—Once the risks are identified, the nature and sources of the risks must be determined in order to assess potential mitigative actions. Such sources may be commercial, legal, technological, political, criminal, managerial, or events of nature (the so-called force majeure).
- Risk evaluation—The final assessment consists of the ability (or lack thereof) to tolerate or accept a given level of risk. Intolerable or unacceptable risks require a plan for mitigation.

Operational risk

Operational risk can be described as any risk resulting from improperly functioning processes, systems, and people. It is, in effect, the risk that occurs from the fallibility of humans and is the residual after considering the more specific financial, systemic, and market risks. An oil refinery technician who fails to properly close a valve, causing a catastrophic plant shutdown and loss of output, is an example of an operational risk. Pilot error leading to the crash of an airliner is another example of operational risk.

Business continuity

The Business Continuity Institute defines business continuity as a process that "identifies potential impacts that threaten an organization and provides a framework for building resilience and the capability for an effective response thereby safeguarding the interests of its key stakeholders, reputation, brand and value-creating activities." In effect, business continuity is a form of risk mitigation designed to protect against the potential disruption of business operations from unforeseen events.

Systemic risk

Systemic risk occurs when entities are operationally interconnected such that the disruption of any single entity creates concomitant effects on other entities (i.e., a ripple effect). Systemic risk is particularly important given the intricate supply chain structure of global manufacturers. For example, severe flooding in the fall of 2011 caused the suspension of hard disk production in Thailand (representing roughly 40% of total worldwide production), which systemically, led to major production disruptions for personal computer manufacturers throughout the world.

Hazard risk

A hazard, simply defined, is any object or event, foreseeable or not, that can lead to injury or loss. Hazard risk is the effect of the uncertainty from not knowing when or if a hazard may occur. Hazard risk can be quantified by determining the probability of occurrence and the magnitude of potential loss. For example, the process of extracting minerals from underground can be considered a workplace hazard. The specific hazard may involve a tunnel collapse, and the harm caused by the hazard is injury or death to workers, economic loss due to business disruption, and financial loss due to the settlement of claims. The magnitude and effect of a particular risk can be viewed as a function of the type of hazard and the vulnerability to the hazard. For example, a tornado is a type of hazard, and tornados occur frequently in the state of Kansas. Therefore, a business operating in Kansas can be considered to be vulnerable to a potential tornado, and a risk exists that such a business can suffer harm. However, because tornados are extremely rare in the state of California, the same business operating in California can be considered to not be vulnerable to a tornado. Therefore, there is little risk.

<u>Risk assessment models to categorize and prioritize hazard risk management</u>
Two commonly cited models of risk management are the history, vulnerability, maximum threat, and Probability (HVMP) model used by the U.S. Federal Emergency Management Agency (FEMA) and the seriousness, manageability, urgency, and growth (SMUG) model developed by the Australian Natural Disasters Organization. Both methods tend to product similar results.
- HVMP—For each risk, the four factors of history, vulnerability, maximum threat, and probability are assigned a score and a weighting factor, the product and summary of which are the quantified threat level; the higher the score, the higher the risk.
- SMUG—Each risk is assessed using four factors: seriousness, manageability, urgency, and growth. Similar to the FEMA model, each factor is assigned a qualitative score of high, medium, and low and then assigned a numerical score. The sum of the individual scores represents the quantified threat level; again, the higher the score, the higher the risk.

Financial risk

A risk is considered to be financial if the uncertainty of an event can be expected to adversely affect the financial structure of an entity. Bankruptcy can be considered a financial risk because the effect of the event is a restructuring of the finances of the debtor, which in turn, will create losses for the creditors and shareholders. Certain financial ratios can provide an indication of the financial risk of a company. The debt ratio, or debt to total assets ratio, measures the relative size of debt in relation to the equity or assets of a company; the higher the ratio, the higher the level of debt and, by extension, the greater the financial risk. A corollary to the debt ratio is the times interest earned ratio, reflecting the ability of a company to service the existing debt. In this case, the lower the ratio, the greater the financial risk.

Risk mitigation strategy

A risk mitigation strategy involves assessing the risks that may potentially affect a company and taking actions to modify the risk itself or modify the potential effects of the risk. The mitigation may take the form of plans (emergency preparedness, business continuity, or facility evacuation), the training of employees (what to do in the event of an earthquake), investment (redundant power supplies and backup facilities) and preventative measures (hardened buildings, shatterproof glass, and security systems).

Strategic risk

The strategic risk of a company is a function of the congruence of the business plan, strategies, and operations with its resources and ability to execute the strategy. The specific risk is the relative level of uncertainty underlying achievement of favorable business results reflected in measures such as revenue, net income, earnings per share, share price, and growth. A company that adopts reasonable strategic initiatives of moderate difficulty, performs effective due diligence with respect to planning, and has a demonstrated history of past achievement and a high level of management commitment can be said to have a lower level of strategic risk. Conversely, a company lacking a record of past achievement that enters into aggressive strategic initiatives without effective planning and analysis and without a high degree of management commitment and direction can be said to have a higher level of strategic risk.

Integrating risk into strategic planning process

The necessity of and benefit from integrating risk into the strategic planning process is best demonstrated by examining the often-used phrase *risk versus reward* or *risk–return ratio*. Broadly used, the phrase indicates that each available reward is accompanied by a level of risk. A rational person can be expected to choose only those rewards that exceed the companion risk by an acceptable amount. Strategic planning in a company is a process that has as its objective the establishment of priorities, determination of initiatives, and allocation of resources in order to achieve future success as measured by the financial return to the owners. As all returns are accompanied by risk, such risk must be assessed to evaluate whether the return from the initiative is sufficient to justify the uncertainty of success.

Options to companies regarding mitigation of risk

Risk mitigation is a process that involves assessing a risk and taking actions to modify the risk itself or the potential effects of the risk. Such actions would be intended to do one of the following:
- Avoid the risk.
- Reduce the risk.
- Eliminate the risk.

- Change the consequences of the risk.
- Change the probabilities of the risk.
- Ignore the risk.

In some cases, it may be desirable to actually increase the risk if the risk is consequential to the exploitation of an opportunity.

ERM

The Committee of Sponsoring Organizations (COSO) consists of representatives from various accounting and financial professional organizations. The mission of the committee is to provide thought leadership on various issues faced by business entities, including risk management. COSO developed their concept of enterprise risk management (ERM) as a framework for integrating the entire universe of risks that must be assessed by an enterprise. In this sense, ERM is defined by COSO as follows:

Enterprise risk management is a process, affected by the entity's board of directors, management, and other personnel, applied in a strategy setting and across the enterprise, designed to identify potential events that may affect the entity, and manage risk to be within the risk appetite, to provide reasonable assurance regarding the achievement of entity objectives.

ERM vs. traditional risk management

Traditional risk management consists of assessing risks individually (i.e., in separate silos) without proper consideration for the systemic effect on an entity. For example, the assessment of risks such as hazard, financial, technological, and operational would be conducted by functional individuals in each silo focused on the separate effect of the specific risk on the enterprise. In contrast, ERM views all risks as systemic across an enterprise and views the potential effects in an aggregate or holistic manner rather than as separate, unrelated events.

Investment Decisions

Developing capital budgets

Capital budgeting is the process of evaluating and selecting capital expenditures. Capital expenditures are the purchase of long-term assets that create a benefit to an organization for a period of more than one year. The process involves generating ideas for capital expenditures, evaluating each possible expenditure, selecting which expenditure to pursue, and performing follow-up to see if the expenditure is creating the expected benefit. Reasons to consider a capital expenditure include replacing existing facilities, expanding facilities, upgrading facilities, or to give the organization a strategic advantage in the market.

Discounted cash flow analysis to calculate value

Before an investment can be valued, a forecast period must first be selected. This forecast period is the duration of time that the investment will earn a cash flow in excess of the investment cost. Once the forecasting period is selected, the revenue growth needs to be determined. Revenue growth is the future sales and profit margins. These figures are then discounted. The discount rate depends on a risk-free interest rate.

Time value of money

The time value of money assumes that money is worth more in the future than it is worth at the present because of its earning potential. It presumes that money invested at the present will produce additional money in the form of profits or interest in the future. Because money needs to be spent before it can produce an income, money has more value the sooner it can create an income. This timing determines the amount of profit the money will produce. The time value of money takes into consideration the future value of money invested at the present and the present value of money to be received in the future.

Forecasting cash flows on capital projects

When making a capital investment decision, an organization needs to determine how long the project or product will return an amount that is greater than the cost of capital. This is the time period that is considered when using discounted cash flow methods to value a project. The organization also needs to look at their competitive and market positions. A rule of thumb to follow is that slow-growing organizations should use a 1 year forecast period. Solid organizations with a proven sales record should use a 5 year forecast period. Organizations going through a growth period and that are in a dominant market position could forecast as many as 10 years out.

Cash flows relevant to making capital investment decision

Only cash flows that are associated with a proposed project are relevant to a decision. Relevant cash flows are those cash flows that result in a change to the organization's existing cash flow. These are the incremental cash flows associated with the project. Only those cash flows that occur after the project is undertaken are relevant. Relevant cash flows include the opportunity costs involved in choosing one project over another, any lost cash flows associated with a reduction of revenue from the downsizing or abandonment of an existing project, any reductions in net working capital involved in investing in a project, and cash outflows due to the payment of financing costs.

Discounted cash flow analysis

Discounted cash flow analysis is a capital budgeting method that looks at the income and costs of an activity, project, or investment and evaluates each to come up with a present value. It takes into consideration the flow of future cash income, the risk involved, and the timing of the cash flow. Because income is received over time, the further out the cash inflow, the higher the discount rate. Discounted cash flow analysis is most often used to value a business. A business is valued according to its forecasted cash flow over a future period of time. This forecasted cash flow is then discounted into a present value. In order to do a proper valuation, one must understand the business, its competition, and its market.

Setting discount rate
When setting a discount rate, the risk involved in the project or investment must be considered. When risk is high, the expected rate of return needs to be high. The size of the organization must be considered. Larger organizations return a lower rate of return. The amount of time that the investment will be held should be considered. The longer the holding period, the higher the rate of return. The debt to equity ratio should be considered. The amount of debt and equity plays a role in the cost of capital. The current market interest rate may be a factor that sets the discount rate. Discount rates should be set using after-tax costs if the cash flow is calculated at an after-tax basis.

Assumptions
There are four assumptions to be considered when using discounted cash flow analysis. Cash flows are computed as if they occur at the end of the year. Discounted cash flow analysis does not consider that cash flows are received at different times during the year. Cash flows are treated as though they are expected and guaranteed when in reality cash flows are projected and are just an estimate of what the organization expects to receive. Cash flows are assumed to be reinvested in the organization, whether in other projects or investments. Discounted cash flow analysis also assumes that the capital markets operate smoothly and with consistency.

Effects of income taxes on cash flows

When a project is discontinued and the assets associated with the project are sold, the proceeds for the sale may be taxed. The amount of taxes depends on the amount of the proceeds, the initial investment in the project's assets, and the book value of the project's assets. When assets are sold at book value, there is no tax effect. If assets are sold at less than book value, the organization incurs a loss and may result in a tax savings. When assets are sold for more than book value, the organization will incur a tax because of the recapture of depreciation.

Internal rate of return

Internal rate of return is a method used by an organization to help decide if a long-term investment should be made. The internal rate of return is a discount rate that has a result of a net present value of zero. This discount rate can be interpreted as being the expected return on the investment. The internal rate of return should be higher than the cost of capital for the investment to be profitable to the organization.

<u>Advantages and disadvantages</u>
An advantage of using internal rate of return is that it takes the time value of money into account and provides a realistic expected rate of return. Internal rate of return should only be used to determine the feasibility of investing in a single project. It does not provide an accurate measure when considering several projects simultaneously. Also, internal rate of return should not be used on projects where the project starts with a sizeable initial cash inflow followed by negative cash flow. In most of these instances, internal rate of return will be lower than the actual rate of return.

Net present value

Net present value is a method used to evaluate which long-term project an organization should undertake. Net present value looks at the size and timing of future cash flows from a project and then discounts these cash flows to come up with a number that represents what the cash flow would be in present dollars. The discount rate is critical when computing net present value. The discount rate should be the minimum acceptable return on the investment and takes into account the risk involved in the investment. This risk is determined by the volatility of the future cash flows. To estimate the discount rate, capital asset pricing models and weighted average cost of capital should be used. In order for net present value to provide a measure of the cash flows that will result from a project, there are rules that must be followed. When calculating cash flow, the inflow and outflow of cash must be used, not accounting variables. Cash flow should be computed on a after-tax basis. In addition to using an after-tax cash flow, the discount rate used must also be computed on an after-tax basis. In addition, all of the real options associated with a project must be identified and these real options must be evaluated once the project has been started. In some cases, internal rate of return is easier to interpret than net present value. The most common cases are mortgages and bonds. Mortgages provide one cash inflow and a series of cash outflows. Internal rate of return makes sense in this case because of the consistent cash flow pattern and a stable repayment schedule. Bonds follow the same pattern. Internal rate of return works when comparing bonds with identical yields and terms.

Weighted average cost of capital for investment purposes

The weighted average cost of capital is a method that helps an organization decide whether or not to invest in a project by acquiring additional capital, whether debt or equity. Weighted average cost of capital is used to measure the cost of capital for a project. It is the minimum rate of return at which a project returns value to the organization. It is a calculation of the value of an organization's capital sources and the expected cost of acquiring additional capital. These capital sources are common stock, preferred stock, bonds, and long-term debt. To arrive at this calculation, the cost of each capital source is multiplied by its proportional share in the total cost of capital and then adding these values together. This calculation shows the organization how much interest it pays for money it finances. The weighted average cost of capital is used to determine if a project is feasible and sets the discount rate to use when determining the net present value of cash flows for a project being considered.

Capital investment

A capital investment is made when an organization purchases an asset that will be used on a long-term basis. The purpose of making a capital investment is to earn a return on the funds spent. When deciding whether to make a capital investment, an organization needs to consider the amount of money to be invested, when the money needs to be spent, and the risk level of the investment. These factors are what determine the expected rate of return.

Capital investment decisions

Capital investment decisions are long-term decisions made by an organization to decide which projects should be undertaken and how much should be invested in those projects. Capital investment decisions also include how an organization should finance a project. The choices are usually with debt financing or with equity financing. If an organization chooses to finance a project by selling equity in the corporation, it also needs to decide whether or not to pay a dividend to its investors. Capital investment decisions are based on financing fixed assets and the capital structure of the financing. These decisions should only be pursued when the project maximizes the benefit to the firm in the way of profits and value. This means that a project should have a positive net present value. The net present value calculation must be applied using an appropriate discount rate. The project also needs to return a positive cash flow. This cash flow should be significant enough to provide a return to those who funded the project in the form of interest payments or dividends.

Factors
When making a capital investment decision, the rate of return for the investment needs to be taken into account. The rate of return is dependent upon the amount, timing, risk, and time value of money. The amount is how much money the investment is expected to return. This amount is usually expressed as a percentage. The timing is length of time that will elapse until the money will be repaid. The sooner the money is repaid, the higher the rate of return. The risk depends on how likely it is that the money will be repaid at the expected rate, within the expected time period, and whether or not the money will be repaid at all. The time value of money takes the present value of the future income into consideration. With riskier investments, the present value of the money returned in the future is less than the current value of the money.

Steps
There are three steps involved in making a capital investment decision: generating ideas for capital investments, classifying these investments, and evaluating each investment. Capital investment decisions are usually made because an organization wants to operate differently or more efficiently. This may entail adding a new product, acquiring another business, expanding facilities, or upgrading equipment. Capital investments are classified according to required maintenance costs, cost savings, revenue generation, expansion capacity, new product introduction, and required projects.

Valuation of projects
Projects are valued using the discounted cash flow and net present value methods. The project with the highest value is the one that should be selected. Valuation is performed by determining the amount and timing of all cash flows projected for each of the projects under consideration. These cash flows are discounted to their present value. To make the right

decision, it is important that the right discount rate is used. This discount rate should reflect the risk involved in the project and the type of financing to be used.

<u>Effects of financing</u>
Capital investment decisions must be financed appropriately. Capital investment financing affects an organization's cash flow and contributes to the risk involved with the long-term viability of the organization. Capital investment financing is a mix of debt and equity financing. Debt financing is a liability to the organization which affects the organization's overall cash flow. Debt financing requires that the organization pay interest payment to service the debt. The organization also needs to repay the principal amount of the debt financed within a specified period of time. Equity financing does not produce the risk involved with debt financing. But, equity financing means that the owners of the organization will have a smaller percentage of ownership after the equity financing has occurred. In most cases, the cost of equity financing is higher than the cost of debt financing.

Payback period

The payback period is the amount of time it takes to recover the cost of an investment. It is the cost of the project divided by the annual cash inflows. The payback method assumes that annual cash inflows are equal from year to year. If the annual cash flows are not equal, a trial and error method needs to be assumed to come up with an estimated payback period. When comparing two or more projects or investments, the better choice is the investment or project with the shortest payback period. It assumes that with shorter payback periods there is more liquidity and less risk.

<u>Discounted payback period and bailout payback period</u>
Discounted payback period is the amount of time it takes to recoup the initial investment made in a project based on the discounted future cash inflow. In other words, the discounted payback period is the amount of time it takes to recoup the initial investment when using the present value of future cash inflows. Bailout payback period is the amount of time it takes to return the investment made in a project when using cash inflows and the salvage value of the project's assets into the calculation.

Advantages and disadvantages of payback method

The advantages of using the payback method are that it takes into account the risk involved in investing in a project. The disadvantages of using the payback method are that it does not take the time value of money into consideration, cash flows that occur after the payback period are not included in the calculation, and it does not factor in the scale or size of the investment. Payback method is not a true measure of profitability like net present value, internal rate of return, or discounted cash flow.

Profitability index

The profitability index is the ranking of projects or investments that are being considered when funds are limited and the number of new projects and investments must be kept under a certain dollar amount. The profitability index determines the relationship between costs and benefits by dividing the present value of future cash flows by the initial investment. When the profitability index is lower than 1.0, the investment present value is less than the initial cash outlay. The higher the profitability index, the more desirable the proposed investment.

Comparing projects of unequal scale and unequal lives

When projects have an unequal scale, for example, when one project has a lower operating cost than another project, the project with the lower operating cost will have a higher net cash flow. If the internal rate of return method is used to evaluate the two projects, the internal rate of return will only measure the profitability of the project based on the dollar invested. Internal rate of return does not measure absolute profitability. When the term structure is not uniform, the internal rate of return method may show a positive return while the net present value method may show a negative return. In this case, internal rate of return is not a meaningful valuation.

Risk

Risk is the possibility that an investment will return an amount that is different from what was expected. It is a measure of the volatility of return on investment. Risk is most times referred to as being the loss of some or all of the principal invested. But, risk also includes the possibility that an investment will perform better than expected. The rule of risk is that the greater the level of risk, the higher the amount of return needs to be realized. This higher return is needed as compensation for the high risk.

Risk analysis

Risk analysis is a means to measure the amount of risk involved with investment decisions. Risk is the volatility of expected returns that can be in the form of earnings and cash flow. Risk analysis is used in capital investment decisions because of the large amount of money that is invested in a project and because these projects have a long life span. Risk analysis makes the assumption that the higher the risk, the higher the expected return needs to be in order to compensate for this high level of risk. Risk is measured using standard deviation and coefficient of variation statistics.

Elements
The three elements of risk analysis are risk assessment, risk management, and risk communication. Risk assessment looks at factors that could cause potential harm to an organization, the probability that these factors will cause harm and the consequences if the harm happens. Risk management determines which risk factors need to be managed and develops a plan of action to control those risks. Risk communication is the process of keeping all parts of the organization aware of the risks and those things that need to be done to keep the risk at a minimum level.

Sensitivity analysis

Sensitivity analysis is a method for dealing with wrong decisions. Sensitivity analysis predicts the outcome of a wrong decision by looking at its effects on profits, costs, and sales. Sensitivity analysis also looks at what could happen if conditions related to a decision should change in the future. It can take into account changes that are beyond the control of the organization such as market conditions and fluctuations in the cost of resources. It also can take into account changes that an organization can control such as increasing production capacity and adding a new product line. Sensitivity analysis also allows an organization to look at different decision alternatives by using a what-if approach to decision making.

Disadvantages
Sensitivity analysis has disadvantages that occur with the input of information. Information may be input incorrectly because of measurement errors, lack of information, or poor understanding of the problem or project being addressed.

Scenario analysis

Scenario analysis is a process by which the expected value of a portfolio is estimated over a given period of time. It commonly focuses on what the "worst-case scenario" might be due to an unfavorable event. One of the common ways that an analyst might use scenario analysis is to find the standard deviation of daily or monthly security returns. Then they would find the expected value for the portfolio for two or three standard deviations above and below the average return.

Real options

Real options are the choices that are available when making an investment decision. It is something that an organization will gain by making a certain decision. These options usually pertain to real or tangible assets such as equipment or manufacturing facilities. Real options are also the result of choices. For example, when considering a project, some of the real options may include expansion of a project, reduction of a project, or the abandonment of a project. Real options affect the valuation of potential investments.

Advantages for valuation purposes
Using real options helps an organization think of the possibilities that can be achieved. This creative approach gives the organization the opportunity to think about what assets are at their disposal. It is a tool that can be of benefit when considering new business and investment opportunities. It allows an organization to not only make a decision based on certainty, it allows the organization to add uncertainties into the decision making process.

Disadvantages for valuation purposes
Using real options for valuation purposes is difficult. First an organization needs to list all the scenarios that may develop from each decision choice. When listing scenarios, an organization may not distinguish between what scenarios are possible and what scenarios are doable. Then, a probability rate and a discount rate must be assigned to each scenario. It is not always easy to estimate the probabilities that a scenario will occur. Along with these rates, the organization also needs to project the cash flows it expects from each scenario and then discount these cash flows to present value. Another disadvantage of real options is that they are difficult to value because they are not liquid assets.

Four common real options
The first real option is the ability to vary an organization's output or production methods. These options are used when an organization chooses to change material inputs when, for example, it feels it can get raw materials at a cheaper price. These options are also used when an organization desires to produce difference products from the same production facility. The second real option is the option to abandon a project before the end of its useful

life. In this option, the organization may sell the cash flows that remain and collect a salvage value. These options are used for large capital requirement projects or when a product's acceptance in the marketplace is uncertain. The third real option is to wait and learn before starting a project. This is done when the organization already owns the property or equipment needed to start a project but chooses to wait to put these assets to use until market conditions are favorable to begin the project. These options are used in the exploration for natural resources. The fourth real option is to make follow-on investments to a project. This is done when one project creates options that make it beneficial to engage in other similar projects.

Real options analysis

Real options analysis is a method used in decision making to determine the best action to take. Real options analysis is a way to predict what will happen in the future. The limiting factor of real options analysis is that the quality of the prediction is only as good as the information gathered and how this information is used. Real options analysis also uses some of the same mathematical formulas that are used when evaluating financial options.

Organizations use real options analysis to assign a value to projects and investments that the organization may undertake in the future. It is not always possible to place a monetary value on these options. The organization needs to look at the potential benefit to the organization and use best efforts to place a monetary value on these benefits. Once this value has been determined, it is incorporated into the net present value of the project or investment.

Net present value analysis

Discounted cash flow, also called *net present value analysis,* is a mathematical process that measures the value of an asset based upon the periodic future cash flows that the asset generates. The cash flows are discounted (i.e., reduced) to account for the time value of money. The key factors required for the analysis are as follows:
- Periodic cash flows from the asset.
- Terminal value (remaining value after the cash flow time horizon).
- Discount rate (often the weighted average cost of capital, or WACC).

The result of the calculation is the present value of the future cash flows, which represents the price that would be paid to receive an annuity over a period of time with a given interest rate. The formula for the calculation is as follows:

$$\sum_{p=1}^{n} \frac{CF_p}{(1+i)^p}$$

CF = periodic cash Flow; n = the number of periods; p = each period (1, 2, 3 . . . n); i = discount rate.

Example

Using the example information provided, calculate the net present value (note: a calculator or spreadsheet software is required). Assume a discount rate of 15%.

NET CASH FLOW	PERIOD					
	1	2	3	4	5	Terminal
NET INCOME	$ 550	$ 622	$ 715	$ 885	$ 1,145	
DEPRECIATION & AMORTIZATION	$ 65	$ 74	$ 89	$ 110	$ 155	
Less tax effect of depr. & amort.	$ (39)	$ (44)	$ (53)	$ (66)	$ (93)	
NET DEPRECIATION & AMORTIZATION	$ 26	$ 30	$ 36	$ 44	$ 62	
CAPITAL EXPENDITURE	$ (50)	$ (65)	$ (80)	$ (95)	$ (110)	
NET CASH FLOW	$ 526	$ 587	$ 671	$ 834	$ 1,097	$ 335

Because the cash flows are uneven (unequal from year to year), each year must be discounted separately. The result is as follows:

NET CASH FLOW	PERIOD					
	1	2	3	4	5	Terminal
NET INCOME	$ 550	$ 622	$ 715	$ 885	$ 1,145	
DEPRECIATION & AMORTIZATION	$ 65	$ 74	$ 89	$ 110	$ 155	
Less tax effect of depr. & amort.	$ (39)	$ (44)	$ (53)	$ (66)	$ (93)	
NET DEPRECIATION & AMORTIZATION	$ 26	$ 30	$ 36	$ 44	$ 62	
CAPITAL EXPENDITURE	$ (50)	$ (65)	$ (80)	$ (95)	$ (110)	
NET CASH FLOW	$ 526	$ 587	$ 671	$ 834	$ 1,097	$ 335
DISCOUNT RATE	15%	15%	15%	15%	15%	15%
PRESENT VALUE FACTOR $1/(1+i)^n$	0.870	0.756	0.658	0.572	0.497	0.332
DISCOUNTED CASH FLOW (DCF)	$ 457	$ 444	$ 441	$ 477	$ 545	$ 111
NET PRESENT VALUE ($\sum$ DCF)	$2,475					

Valuation multiples

A valuation multiple represents the quotient of two financial measures (A / B_1) of a company that, when multiplied by the equivalent divisor of a target company (B_2), yields a value of a comparable company. Such multiples are categorized as either enterprise or equity. Enterprise multiples are those in which the financial measures use enterprise value (EV), which is calculated as market capitalization (all classes of stock) plus net debt minus cash:

- EV / EBITDA (earnings before interest, tax, depreciation and amortization)
- EV / EBIT
- EV / sales

Equity multiples are those in which the financial measures are based upon some relationship between market capitalization and actual book value:

- share price / earnings per share (price–earnings ratio)
- share price / book value per share

prospective price–earnings ratio / prospective average earnings growth

- 93 -

Enterprise value

Enterprise value in principle represents the price that must be paid in order to acquire a stock corporation. The acquiring company would be expected to compensate shareholders based upon the market value of their holdings, including holders of preferred issues as well as minority interests. In addition, security holders (non-trade creditors) would also need to be compensated for the value of outstanding debt. The total amount to be paid to all equity and debt holders represents the value of the enterprise. For example, using the enterprise multiple based upon EV / EBIT, the value of a comparable company would be calculated as follows:

ENTERPRISE VALUE:			ENTERPRISE MULTIPLE USING EBIT:		
COMMON SHARES	$	60,500	ENTERPRISE VALUE	$	62,487
PREFERRED SHARES	$	12,600	EBIT	$	4,277
MINORITY INTEREST	$	3,775	**MULTIPLE (EV/EBIT)**		**14.6**
TOTAL DEBT	$	12,740	COMPARABLE COMPANY EBIT	$	2,270
CASH	$	(27,128)	COMPARABLE COMPANY VALUE	$	33,165
	$	62,487			

Operation of an asset-based model used for valuation of potential acquisition

An asset-based model uses the valuation of the assets (such as the liquidation value or replacement value) as the measure of the overall entity value (and thus the acquisition price). While the method may entail significant challenges and complexities with regard to assessing the fair value of the assets, the method is appropriate for asset-intensive firms that have marginal or negative earnings (rendering the discounted cash flow approach infeasible) or a low stock price (yielding a poor result using the relative approach).

DCF used for valuation of potential acquisition

The discounted cash flow (DCF) approach consists of a mathematical determination of the net present value of the future income stream (or cash flow) of a potential acquisition. The formula incorporates the variables of income or cash per period (usually years), the number of periods to be considered, and an appropriate discount rate, typically the required rate of return. The calculation will deliver a result that can be understood as the amount to be paid in the present for an annuity extending into the future.

A simplified example is as follows:

NET CASH FLOW	PERIOD					
	1	2	3	4	5	Terminal
NET INCOME	$ 550	$ 622	$ 715	$ 885	$ 1,145	
DEPRECIATION & AMORTIZATION	$ 65	$ 74	$ 89	$ 110	$ 155	
Less tax effect of depr. & amort.	$ (39)	$ (44)	$ (53)	$ (66)	$ (93)	
NET DEPRECIATION & AMORTIZATION	$ 26	$ 30	$ 36	$ 44	$ 62	
CAPITAL EXPENDITURE	$ (50)	$ (65)	$ (80)	$ (95)	$ (110)	
NET CASH FLOW	$ 526	$ 587	$ 671	$ 834	$ 1,097	$ 335
DISCOUNT RATE	25%	25%	25%	25%	25%	25%
PRESENT VALUE FACTOR $1/(1+i)^n$	0.800	0.640	0.512	0.410	0.328	0.247
DISCOUNTED CASH FLOW (DCF)	$ 421	$ 375	$ 343	$ 342	$ 359	$ 83

NET PRESENT VALUE (Σ DCF)

$$\boxed{\$1,923}$$

value of the acquisition

Relative model used for valuation of potential acquisition

The relative value approach (also called the *market approach*) uses key factors and measures (typically multiples) of comparable companies in order to determine the value of the target company. The critical success factor with this method is identifying the appropriate comparable companies and applying the appropriate measures. For example, for a potential acquisition company that manufactures and distributes appliances, the appropriate comparable would logically be another such manufacturer and distributor combination. However, if the information for such a comparison is not publicly available, the comparable company could be viewed separately as comparisons to other manufacturers and comparisons to other distributors. The appropriate measures, typically enterprise or equity multiples, depend upon the nature of the business and the industry within which it operates. For example, a rapidly growing company might require the use of the price earnings to growth (PEG) ratio.

Discount rate used in DCF modeling

The discount rate to be used in DCF analysis is dependent upon the nature of the periodic cash flow or income stream. For example, an analysis of cash flows resulting from a potential equipment acquisition would use a discount rate that reflects the appropriate cost of capital. If the equipment is to be financed through borrowing, the discount rate would be the cost of debt. As an additional example, assume a company is considering purchasing a subsidiary of another company and plans to issue additional shares to the public, combined with bank borrowing. The discount rate most applicable in this case would be the weighted average cost of capital (WACC), which considers both debt and equity. Finally, assume the same company purchasing the subsidiary has the cash on hand with which to make the purchase. Assuming the company has other investing opportunities available, an appropriate discount rate in this case would be the best return available from those other opportunities.

WACC

The Weighted average cost of capital (WACC) calculation is intended to create a single average measure, expressed as a percentage, of the cost of all sources of capital available to a company, both debt and equity. The cost of debt capital is typically fairly straightforward, consisting of the average interest rate (or yield to maturity in the case of bonds), either stated or implied and adjusted for taxes. The calculation is expressed as the rate multiplied by one minus the tax rate. The cost of equity capital is a bit more complex and often requires the use of the capital asset pricing model (CAPM). This model considers the risk-free rate of return available to investors (typically a U.S. government security) adjusted for the market and equity risk premiums required to hold stock. The calculation is expressed as follows:

Risk free rate + (market risk multiple × equity risk)

The individual components are then weighted based upon the proportion of each in the capital structure.

<u>Example</u>
Using the example information provided, calculate the weighted average cost of capital (WACC).

COMPONENTS OF WACC CALCULATION:

TOTAL ASSETS	$ 30,000	AVERAGE INTEREST RATE	**6.50%**	FROM COMPANY INFORMATION
TOTAL DEBT	$ 12,000	RISK FREE RATE OF RETURN	2.50%	10 YR U.S. TREASURY NOTE
TOTAL EQUITY	$ 18,000	MARKET RISK BETA	1.45	FROM PUBLIC SOURCES
TOTAL DEBT & EQUITY	$ 30,000	EQUITY RISK PREMIUM	5.00%	HISTORICAL DATA

The calculation of WACC is as follows:

COST OF EQUITY CAPITAL: **9.75%**   RISK FREE + (BETA X EQUITY PREMIUM)

CALCULATION OF WACC:

CAPITAL STRUCTURE		CAPITAL COST		WEIGHTED AVERAGE	
DEBT	40%	DEBT	6.50%	DEBT	2.60%
EQUITY	60%	EQUITY	9.75%	EQUITY	5.85%
				WACC	**8.45%**

Capital investment decision

An organization makes capital investment decisions when deciding to increase their manufacturing facilities and when deciding to replace existing facilities. When an organization decides to increase facilities it will need to make an investment in property, manufacturing plant, and equipment. In addition, it needs to decide how it will handle the additional sales and what it will need to invest in product development, market research, and restructuring debt. Replacing existing facilities may require that the organization decide on a new computer system, new machinery and equipment, or upgrading and remodeling a building.

Capital budgeting

Capital budgeting is a method used to help an organization decide if a long-term project or investment will be feasible and profitable. Types of long-term projects and investments may include purchasing new or replacement equipment, adding a new product to production, or moving to a new production facility. It uses discounted cash flow methods, internal rates of return calculations, net present value methods, and payback periods to help make this decision. Capital budgeting requires that an organization look at the various costs and benefits involved in each of the investment alternatives being considered. It is important to consider capital budgeting decisions carefully because they play a major role in an organization's long-term profitability.

Capital budgeting to make decisions
Capital budgeting is the process of assigning a value to the cash flow to be realized from a project to be undertaken or from the purchase of a real asset. The cash flow for a project or an asset being considered is from the time of acquisition until the end of the project or life of the asset. Once the cash flow is determined, it is discounted to its present value. Also considered in the capital budgeting process is the net investment for the organization. The net investment is the cost of the project plus any installation costs less any proceeds from the disposal of the project.

Professional Ethics

Ethics

Ethics are a set of rules of duty or rules of practice that govern human actions. Ethics are a set of standards that determine whether human actions are right or wrong. Ethics establish standards of conduct for a single individual or for a group of individuals. When ethics are applied to a group, the ethics are the obligations and duties that the group requires that the individual members adhere to. The purpose of ethical standards is to ensure that actions are accomplished for the advancement of the common good or the common goal. To regulate member behavior, many organizations have developed a code of ethics. A code of ethics outlines the standards of behavior that the members of the organization will follow regarding their moral and professional obligations toward one another, their clients, and society.

Scope of the Institute of Management Accountants Statement of Ethical Professional Practice

The Institute of Management Accountants Statement of Ethical Professional Practice contains four principles that all management accountants will adhere to, four standards that guide ethical behavior of management accountants, and outlines the actions to be taken when there are ethical conflicts. The purpose of the Statement of Ethical Professional Practice is to guide management accountants in the behavior appropriate to ethical behavior and to inform of the values of the organization. The four principles include honesty, fairness, objectivity, and responsibility. These principles are the values that the organization puts forth as being important for its members. The four standards include competence, confidentiality, integrity, and credibility. The standards outline the behavior expected of the membership.

Institute of Management Accountants standards

Confidentiality standards
There are three areas where a management accountant must demonstrate confidentiality. The management accountant is required to keep all information confidential. The only exception to this rule is when disclosure of the information must be made available when authorized by the owner of the information or under legal requests. The management accountant must inform subordinates and other concerned individuals that information is to be kept confidential and on how confidential information must be appropriately used. The management accountant is also responsible for overseeing subordinates and ensuring that they comply with the confidentiality rules. The management accountant is prohibited from using confidential information for any unethical means or to obtain illegal advantage.

Competency standards
There are four areas where a management accountant must demonstrate competency. The management accountant has the responsibility to continually work toward developing their knowledge and skills. This enables the management accountant to maintain their level of professional expertise. The management accountant has the responsibility to perform their job in compliance with relevant laws, regulations, and technical standards. The

management accountant must provide decision support information and recommendations so that the information provided is clear, concise, accurate, and timely. The management accountant is responsible for performing activities responsibly and for good judgment. It is also their responsibility to inform others of any conditions or professional limitations that would preclude them from acting responsibly and with good judgment.

Credibility standards

There are three areas where a management accountant must demonstrate credibility. When a management accountant provides information to a client or to the public, it must be communicated in a manner that is fair and objective. Full disclosure is of prime importance. The management accountant must disclose all of the information that the client or the public needs in order to make a decision. The information provided must enable the client or public to fully understand the reports, analyses, and recommendations provided by the management accountant. The management accountant must ensure that the information provided is in accordance with organizational policy and applicable laws. Any activity or information that does not conform to organizational policy and applicable laws must be disclosed. This may include delays in presenting the information, deficiencies in the information, timeliness of the information, or problems with internal controls.

Integrity standards

There are three areas where a management accountant must demonstrate integrity. It is the responsibility of the management accountant to avoid the possibility of any conflicts of interest. If there is a possibility of a conflict of interest, the management accountant must inform all parties involved of the conflict and must mitigate any actual conflicts of interest. The management accountant must avoid any action or activity that prevents them from performing their duties and functions in an ethical manner. The management accountant must abstain from any activity or conduct that would have a detrimental effect on the accounting profession. The management accountant must also abstain from supporting those activities that would discredit other members of the organization or the organization itself.

Business Ethics Advisory Council

The Business Ethics Advisory Council was formed in 1961 as a responsibility of the Secretary of Commerce. The Business Ethics Advisory Council was created in response to the electrical equipment conspiracy cases in 1960. Recommendations made by the Business Ethics Advisory Council caused large organizations to become aware of the problems associated with unethical behavior. The Business Ethics Advisory Council found several ethical areas that needed to be addressed by organizations: 1) businesses needed a better understanding of ethical issues, 2) businesses needed a way in which to better comply with laws, 3) activities that were a conflict of interest between the business and its clients and the public needed to be addresses, 4) abuse of entertainment and gift expenses needed to be addressed, 5) proper behavior for customer and supplier relationships needed to be addressed, and 6) businesses have a responsibility to society.

Code of ethics

A code of ethics outlines an organization's values, rules of conduct, and the penalties for not adhering to the organization's ethical standards. The code of ethics is intended to set the tone for the code of professional responsibility that the members of an organization are

- 99 -

required to follow in order to maintain their membership or standing in the organization. The code of ethics also outlines the procedures that are followed to determine whether or not a violation of the code of ethics has occurred. It also indicates the type of remedy or penalty that should be imposed when there is a violation. When a member is in violation of the code of ethics, the member may be subject to administrative, civil, or penal penalties.

A code of ethics communicates an organization's purpose, values, and beliefs. Its intent is to guide the members of the organization toward the proper behavior when dealing with employees, customers, and the public. When a code of ethics is communicated to all members of the organization, all of the members of the organization understand what behavior is expected of them. A code of ethics establishes standards that allow members to assess and measure their performance. A code of ethics also communicates the organization's purpose and values to the public. A code of ethics informs the members of the organization about the disciplinary actions, penalties, and punishment that will be levied upon a member if the member fails to adhere to ethical standards. In addition, these penalties are made known to clients and the public.

Behaviors that may lead to unethical behavior

The reasons for unethical behavior in the workplace are as varied as the individuals employed by an organization. Organizational goals and standards may lead to unethical behavior. If managers and employees feel pressured to attain goals and standards, they may falsely submit records that do not accurately represent the work performed. The expectation of reaching a specified return on investment may lead to financial records being manipulated in such a way as to show a higher return. This is known as "cooking the books." Personality conflicts may lead to unethical behavior. When a subordinate lacks respect or confidence in a superior, that subordinate may take actions that undermine the superior's authority. When decisions are made by committee, there is room for unethical behavior. In the decision making process, one or more individuals may unreasonably influence the group to vote in their favor and not in the best interest of the organization. Competition can also lead to unethical behavior. In order to generate sales, an individual or organization may revert to bribes or untruthful sales practices in order to obtain customers and revenues.

Sarbanes-Oxley Act of 2002 reforms

The Sarbanes-Oxley Act was a result of the Enron scandal and other improper business practices committed by large organizations in 2001 and 2002. The Sarbanes-Oxley Act introduced reforms in the areas of corporate responsibility, criminal penalties, accounting regulation, and securities protection. Corporate officers became accountable for certifying the accuracy of financial reports, were prohibited from selling company stock under certain conditions, required to report sales of stock trades, unable to take out company loans if those loans were not also available to company outsiders, and make immediate disclosure of material changes in a company's financial condition. The penalties for destroying or altering company records, defrauding shareholders, and filing false financial reports were increased. Auditors became regulated by an oversight board. The statute of limitations for securities fraud was extended and provided protection for whistle-blowers and financial analysts.

Resolving ethical conduct

When a management accountant encounters an instance of unethical behavior, the first course of action is to follow the organization's established rules for resolving ethical conduct. If following this method does not provide a solution to the problem, the management accountant is obligated to take the issue to their immediate supervisor. If the immediate supervisor appears to be involved in the ethical conflict, the management accountant should take the issue to the next level of management. When the immediate supervisor is an upper or executive level manager, the issue may be taken to a review or audit committee, the board of directors, or the owners of the organization. Resolution of ethical conduct issues should be handled within the organization. It is not appropriate to take the issue outside the organization unless there is a violation of a law or regulation. If a management accountant is unsure of the course of action to take, the matter should be discussed with an Institute of Management Accountants ethics counselor or with a legal attorney.

Corporate social responsibility

Corporate social responsibility is the obligation of the organization to act in a way in which the welfare of the organization and of society is protected and improved. Corporate social responsibility strives to attain both organizational goals and societal goals. Organizations can display their socially responsible activities in many ways. Some organizations get involved in improving the living conditions in urban neighborhoods. Some strive to improve the quality of consumer products. Others may get involved in cleaning up the environment. The reasons that organizations get involved in socially responsible activities is that by improving societal conditions the organization will improve conditions within the organization and for the employees that work for the organization. Socially responsible activities also create goodwill for an organization. The goodwill the organization receives from its employees, its customers, and from the community may translate into increased profits and revenues for the organization.

Conflict of interest

A conflict of interest is a situation where an individual has a conflict between their personal life and their professional or fiduciary responsibilities. This conflict causes a situation where the individual will benefit on a personal level because of the knowledge or position obtained in their professional or fiduciary capacity. Because of this conflict, the individual may lack the judgment, independence, or objectivity to make an unbiased decision or render an unbiased opinion or recommendation. A conflict of interest can occur under a number of situations. When a management accountant has a financial interest in a supplier, a customer, or a distributor a conflict of interest may occur because the management accountant may have access to confidential financial information. A conflict of interest can cause others to lose confidence in an individual.

RICO

The Racketeer Influenced and Corrupt Organization Act (RICO) was enacted as a means of punishing organizations that participated in certain types of criminal activities. The original purpose of RICO was to eliminate the proliferation of organized crime in the United States. These racketeering activities include gambling, bribery, extortion, bankruptcy fraud, mail fraud, securities fraud, prostitution, narcotics trafficking, loan sharking, and murder. Under the provisions of RICO, proceeds from racketeering activities cannot be used to purchase an interest in an organization and no individual associated with an organization may conduct racketeering activity through that organization. If convicted of a RICO violation, the individual is fined, sentenced to no more than 20 years in prison, and must forfeit any ownership in the organization in which the racketeering activity was transacted.

Basic ethical behaviors expected of financial manager in regards to accounting activities

A financial manager must uphold several ethical behaviors – avoid conflicts of interest, present financial information fairly and accurately, uphold laws and regulations, and be objective. A financial manager must avoid both conflicts of economic interest and conflicts of professional interest. Shareholders must receive financial information that accurately represents the condition of the corporation and the financial information must not be presented so that it protects management from performance failures. Financial information must be presented to the appropriate members of management and the financial information must be accurate. Financial reports must be prepared in accordance with applicable laws and regulations. If there is any illegal or fraudulent activity within an organization, the financial manager must report the activity to the appropriate authorities. All reports and information must be presented in an objective manner.

FCPA

The Foreign Corrupt Practices Act of 1977 (FCPA) was a result of illegal acts of U.S. organizations committed in foreign nations. Most of these illegal acts were in the form of payments made to foreign governments and political parties. These payments were used to bribe foreign officials and political parties into entering business relationships. These payments may appear in the financial records of an organization as overpayments, missing records, unrecorded transactions, misclassified costs, and retranscription of records. The goal of the FCPA was to restore confidence in the business transactions of U.S. organizations. The FCPA requires that all organizations that fall under the jurisdiction of the Securities and Exchange Commission maintain internal accounting controls and file regular reports to the SEC. The purpose of this is to ensure that transactions are executed and recorded appropriately and that assets are used according to management authorization.

Fraud triangle

The fraud triangle is a model that explains the factors the lead to someone committing occupational fraud. It contains the three components that together will lead to fraudulent behavior:
1. Perceived unshareable financial need
2. Perceived opportunity
3. Rationalization

If someone feels that they are in a financial bind, and they have the opportunity, and they can rationalize to themselves what they are doing then they are more likely to commit fraud.

Practice Test

Practice Questions

1. Which item is not found on a balance sheet?
   a. Deposits
   b. Patents
   c. Taxes paid
   d. Accrued expenses

2. Which item is included in the statement of cash flows?
   a. Investments by shareholders
   b. Net income
   c. Accrued income
   d. Payments made for products and services

3. Which section of a business' financial statements provides details on its liquidity?
   a. Notes to the financial statement
   b. Cash flow statement
   c. Management Discussion and Analysis
   d. Statement of changes in shareholders' equity

4. How is the Acid-Test Ratio computed?
   a. Current assets divided by current liabilities
   b. Cash, accounts receivable, and short-term investments divided by current liabilities
   c. Sales divided by inventory
   d. Accounts payable divided by cost of sales and multiplied by days in accounting period

5. What financial ratio is used to measure an organization's risk?
   a. Debt-to-equity ratio
   b. Current ratio
   c. Acid-Test ratio
   d. Days sales outstanding in receivables

6. Which financial ratio indicates how well an organization's net assets can cover its debt obligations?
   a. Earnings to Fixed Charges ratio
   b. Debt to total assets ratio
   c. Asset Coverage ratio
   d. Times Interest Earned ratio

7. Analyzing a company's return on investment would not necessarily be useful in measuring...
   a. the earning potential of an asset
   b. profitability from operations
   c. how well an organization uses resources
   d. operational efficiency

8. Which three components are used by the DuPont Model to determine return on equity?
   a. Net margin, asset turnover, and return on investment
   b. Net margin, asset turnover, and financial leverage
   c. Cost of investment, asset turnover, and financial leverage
   d. Cost of investment, asset turnover, and solvency

9. Which profit margin calculation gives the best indication of earnings potential?
   a. Gross profit margin
   b. Operating profit margin
   c. Net profit margin
   d. Financing profit margin

10. Multinational corporations protect themselves against foreign currency translation exposure by...
   a. using a standard exchange rate
   b. hiring accountants from their subsidiaries' countries
   c. purchasing materials from foreign nations
   d. preparing consolidated financial statements

11. Which type of trade organization uses a common currency between member nations?
   a. Customs union
   b. Economic union
   c. Common market
   d. Free trade market

12. Which item is NOT considered a change in accounting principles?
   a. Change to accrual accounting
   b. Change in depreciation method
   c. Discontinued operations
   d. Change in inventory method

13. Which of the following variables may help determine rates of return?
   a. Amount of risk
   b. Compounded interest
   c. Book value
   d. Marginal cost of capital

14. What does standard deviation of return measure?
   a. Potential outcome of a gain or loss
   b. Level of risk
   c. Profitability
   d. Investment risk

15. Which financial tool predicts how much an investment's value would decrease over a short time period?
   a. Hedging
   b. Value at Risk
   c. Diversification
   d. Rate of return

16. What type of dividend do corporations most commonly pay to shareholders and bondholders?
    a. Property dividends
    b. Stock dividends
    c. Stock split
    d. Cash dividends

17. Which ratio indicates if a corporation's stock is undervalued or overvalued?
    a. Price/Earnings ratio
    b. Price/Book ratio
    c. Price/Sales ratio
    d. Debt/Equity ratio

18. What financial measurement helps a company decide whether or not to invest in a major financing project?
    a. Rate of return
    b. Debt to equity
    c. Book value
    d. Market value

19. Which condition is NOT true of equity financing?
    a. No obligation to repay the investment
    b. Ease of obtaining financing for small businesses
    c. Assistance by investors
    d. Owners retain same level of control

20. How does an organization facilitate customer payments when it sells products in multiple states?
    a. Lockbox systems
    b. Concentration banking
    c. Electronic commerce
    d. Accounts payable

21. Which inventory model helps a company plan for more inventory to be stocked when levels reach a certain point?
    a. Last in, first out
    b. First in, first out
    c. Periodic review system
    d. Continuous review system

22. What federal legislation provided for the formation of the Securities and Exchange Commission?
    a. Securities Act of 1933
    b. Securities Exchange Act of 1934
    c. Sarbanes-Oxley Act of 2002
    d. Public Company Accounting Oversight Board

23. Which type of opinion is issued once an auditor determines that an organization's financial statements are represented fairly?
    a. Unqualified opinion
    b. Unqualified opinion with explanatory language
    c. Qualified opinion
    d. Disclaimer of opinion

24. Which type of organizational structure is based on performance and project needs?
    a. Functional organization
    b. Matrix organization
    c. Line organization
    d. Line and staff organization

25. Which type of international financing method guarantees payment at face value of the financed amount?
    a. Letter of credit
    b. Forfaiting
    c. Banker's acceptance
    d. Countertrade

26. Which factor is NOT used when performing a cost/volume/profit analysis?
    a. Production volume
    b. Product mix
    c. Fixed costs
    d. Markup percentage

27. Which type of cost can be classified as both a variable cost and fixed cost?
    a. Rent
    b. Cost of goods sold
    c. Labor
    d. Utilities

28. Which of the following is a characteristic of an avoidable cost?
    a. Utilities incurred by discontinuing a product
    b. Material costs incurred by discontinuing a product
    c. Cost of equipment that is considered obsolete
    d. Lost sales from a product not chosen for market

29. Which variable is used when performing marginal analysis?
    a. Excess manufacturing capability
    b. Cost of purchasing product from outside sources
    c. The business cycle of the organization
    d. The opportunity cost associated with the product selection process

30. What is the primary difference in how qualitative and quantitative factors are used in the decision making process?
    a. How the factors are measured
    b. The value of the factors
    c. The unavoidable costs associated with the factors
    d. The effects of changes when a factor fluctuates

31. In the market segmentation process, potential customers are first grouped...
    a. by demographic information
    b. according to products and associated benefits
    c. by need and buying behavior
    d. according to the size of the customer base

32. What is the effect on a product when a surplus in supply exists?
    a. More products will be supplied to the market
    b. The price of the product will increase
    c. The price of the product will stay the same
    d. The price of the product will decrease

33. Which price adjustment strategy offers incentives to customers to help stimulate product sales?
    a. Promotional pricing
    b. Discount and allowance pricing
    c. Psychological pricing
    d. Segmented pricing

34. How is cross elasticity of demand computed?
    a. The percentage change in demand for one product divided by the percentage change in price to a second product
    b. The percentage change in supply divided by the percentage change in price
    c. The percent change in the quantity demanded divided by the percent change in price
    d. The percentage change in quantity divided by the percentage change in price

35. Capital budgeting considers all but which of the following factors?
    a. The cost of the project
    b. The cash flow of a project
    c. The net investment for the organization
    d. The rate of return of the project

36. In forecasting cash flows on capital projects, which time horizon is most sensible for which type of organization?
    a. Five years— for a slow growing company
    b. One year— for a high-growth company
    c. 10 years— for a company that dominates its market
    d. Three years— for a startup business

37. Internal rate of return is a better valuation method than net present value when...
    a. cash flow fluctuates between accounting periods
    b. investing in a project by acquiring additional capital
    c. valuing mortgages and bonds
    d. valuing real estate investments

38. Which capital budgeting method is most often used to determine the value of a business?
    a. Discounted cash flow analysis
    b. Weighted average cost of capital
    c. Internal rate of return
    d. Net present value

39. What assumption can be made when using payback period to compare two or more investments?
    a. Trial and error is used to determine future cash flows
    b. Limits must be set on the amount of investment
    c. Investments with shorter payback periods have more liquidity and less risk
    d. Investments with longer payback periods have more liquidity and more risk

40. Which is NOT a true measure of profitability?
    a. Payback method
    b. Net present value
    c. Internal rate of return
    d. Discounted cash flow

41. Which factor is not considered in a capital investment decision?
    a. Rate of return on the investment
    b. The time period in which the investment will be repaid
    c. The risk that the investment may not be repaid or repaid at the expected rate
    d. Future cash flows received from the investment

42. How are projects and investments valued when making capital investment decisions?
    a. Discounted cash flow and rate of return
    b. Discounted cash flow and net present value
    c. Rate of return and internal rate of return
    d. Net present value and weighted average cost of capital

43. What effect does the financing of capital investments have on a company's future stability and profitability?
    a. Increases risk and decreases rate of return
    b. Decreases risk and decreases control
    c. Increases cash flow and increases risk
    d. Decreases cash flow and increases risk

44. What statistical calculations are used to measure the amount of risk involved with an investment decision?
    a. Net present value and cash equivalent coefficient
    b. Standard deviation and cash equivalent coefficient
    c. Standard deviation and coefficient of variation
    d. Coefficient of variation and net present value

45. Analysts attempt to measure the effect of a wrong decision on a company's profits, costs, and sales by performing...
    a. risk analysis
    b. sensitivity analysis
    c. certainty equivalent
    d. real options analysis

46. What is an advantage of using real options analysis to determine the value of an investment decision?
    a. Determines the volatility of return on the investment
    b. Helps an organization deal with wrong decisions
    c. The investment is measured against risk-free investments
    d. Uncertainties are considered in the decision

47. To whom, or in which document, must a financial manager report an organization's fraudulent activity, once detected?
    a. To the board of directors
    b. To the appropriate authorities
    c. In the financial statements
    d. In the annual report

48. Which of the following behaviors is NOT considered to lead to unethical behavior?
    a. Slight exaggerations on performance evaluations
    b. Disrespect for authority
    c. Whistle blowing
    d. Using untruthful sales practices to generate customers

49. How does the Racketeer Influenced and Corrupt Organizations Act (RICO) prohibit organizations from participating in racketeering activities?
    a. Proceeds from racketeering activities cannot be used to invest in a corporation
    b. Imposes fines and prison terms for racketeering activities
    c. Requires organizations to file reports with the Securities And Exchange Commission
    d. Promotes corporate social responsibility

50. Which federal legislation was enacted as a result of illegal payments made to foreign governments?
    a. Sarbanes-Oxley Act of 2002
    b. Racketeer Influenced and Corrupt Organizations Act
    c. Business Ethics Advisory Council
    d. Foreign Corrupt Practices Act of 1977

Answers and Explanations

1. C: Taxes paid. The balance sheet is a company's financial statement that summarizes assets, liabilities and shareholders' equity. It's most often the starting point for decisions made by the investment and financial communities to determine the scope of an organization's resources, its dependence on external financing, and its adaptability to new business conditions. A balance sheet contains three categories of accounts:
   - Assets— financial resources such as cash, accounts receivable, deposits, inventory, property, patents, and equipment. Assets are categorized as:
      - Current— assets easily convertible to cash
      - Fixed— expected to be retained long-term
   - Liabilities— any obligation including accounts payable, accrued expenses, taxes payable, short-term loans, mortgages, and long-term loans. Liabilities are categorized as:
      - Current— due in a year or less from preparation date of balance sheet
      - Long-term— obligations that take longer than a year to pay off, such as leases and loans
   - Shareholders' equity— the company's net worth, or the difference between assets and liabilities. Equal to the shareholders' contributions (stock) and retained earnings

2. D: Payments made for products and services. A cash flow statement reports the business' cash receipts and payments, classified by:
   - Operating activities— cash received from the sale of products and services, and payments for products and services used in the course of conducting business
   - Investing activities— purchase of property, plant, equipment, and other assets needed to conduct and grow the business
   - Financing activities— money contributed to the business by shareholders or borrowing

Investments by shareholders are found in the statement of changes in shareholder's equity. Net income is found on the income statement, and accrued income is found on the balance sheet.

3. C: Management Discussion and Analysis. The Management Discussion and Analysis (MD&A) is a section of a financial statement containing managerial comment on the business' performance during the period covered by the financial statement. The MD&A addresses the business' financial position, cash flow, liquidity and capital resources, among other things. Most MD&A sections will provide details about short- and long-term goals, new prospects or changes under consideration, and contain information about the business' management and management style.

4. B: Cash, accounts receivable, and short-term investments divided by current liabilities The Acid-Test, or Quick, ratio measures the ability of a business to pay its current liabilities. It is calculated by adding cash, accounts receivable, and short-term investments and then dividing the sum by the current liabilities. Other important metrics that help reveal a company's position with respect to current liabilities:

- Current, or Cash, Ratio— measures ability to pay short-term liabilities using short-term assets, i.e., how quickly it can generate cash. Calculated by dividing current assets by current liabilities
- Inventory turnover— determines how often inventory was replaced over a time period. Calculated by dividing sales by inventory
- Days payable outstanding— measures the length of time a business takes to pay its accounts payable. Calculated by dividing accounts payable by cost of sales and multiplying the result by the number of days in the accounting period

5. A: Debt-To-Equity ratio. As businesses use their capital structures to finance operations, measuring the degree of risk in a business is dependent on measuring the health of the capital structure. The Debt-To-Equity ratio divides total liabilities by shareholders' equity to determine a business' level of risk. A business using more debt will be more risky. The Current ratio and acid test ratio determine how quickly a business can turn products into cash, and how well a business can pay its current liabilities. When the Acid-Test ratio is lower than the Current ratio, it usually indicates the business is invested substantially in inventory. Days sales outstanding in receivables is the average number of days it takes for an organization to collect its accounts receivable. A high number shows weak sales or ineffectiveness in collecting receivables.

6. C: Asset Coverage ratio. The Asset Coverage ratio measures a business' ability to cover its debt obligations with its assets, once all liabilities are satisfied. It's used to determine the extent of potential losses if a business were liquidated. The Earnings To Fixed Charges ratio, also known as the Fixed-Charge Coverage ratio, measures ability to pay fixed financing expenses from profits. The Debt To Total Assets ratio measures financial risk by showing how much of a business' assets have been financed with debt. The Times Interest Earned ratio measures of a business' ability to pay its debt obligations. It shows how many times an organization can cover its interest payments on a pretax basis.

7. D: Operational efficiency. Return on investment (ROI) is normally used to measure the earning potential of an asset or product. Financial professionals use ROI to determine how well an organization utilizes its resources and to determine its financial strength. It can also be used to measure profitability from operations, which, in turn, is a measure of management's effectiveness. ROI would also provide indications of how well a business meets its goals and its competitive position. Profit margin on sales is used to determine operational efficiency, revealing how much income is received for each dollar of sales. Profit margin on sales can also be used to compare the business with competitors or industry peers.

8. B: Net margin, asset turnover, and financial leverage. The DuPont Model, first used within the DuPont Corporation, is used to clarify return on equity (ROE), breaking it down into three components to reveal how a business receives (or the specific sources of) this return. The three components are:
- Net margin— net income divided by sales
- Asset turnover— sales divided by total assets
- Financial leverage— total assets divided by average shareholder equity

The DuPont formula calculates ROE by first calculating the three components, then multiplying them. By separating ROE into these elements, changes in ROE can be tracked over a period of time.

9. A: Gross profit margin. Gross profit margin is the percent of sales dollars that are not spent on expenses. It's calculated by dividing gross income by net sales. Gross profit margin is considered a better indication of earnings potential than just looking at earnings alone, since an earnings increase may not always be accompanied by a profit margin increase. A higher gross profit margin indicates a higher amount of money left over after a business pays its expenses, in turn indicating that this business is demonstrating good control over its costs. When an organization's costs have increased at a greater rate than earnings, the gross profit margin will go down. Operating profit margin is also known as return on sales, and helps measure operational efficiency. Net profit margin measures the proportion of revenue retained after paying variable production costs.

10. D: Preparing consolidated financial statements. Foreign currency translation exposure is the risk that the exchange rate conversions would alter the value of assets, liabilities, equity, or income. A multinational corporation can reduce this risk by using consolidation techniques for its financial statements. Consolidated financial statements are financial statements that include the accounting records of a multinational business' subsidiaries into the corporation's accounting records, resulting in one comprehensive financial statement. Another method to curtail the currency translation exposure risk is to use effective cost accounting evaluation procedures. The foreign currency translation exposure is recorded in the financial statements as either an exchange rate gain or an exchange rate loss.

11. B: Economic union. An economic union is an organization of nations sharing a common currency. A customs union is an organization of nations that has agreed to eliminate customs restrictions between members, and to impose a uniform tariff with non-members. A common market is an organization of nations formed to facilitate trade, and reduce regulatory requirements and trade barriers between members. Free trade is trade between nations without protective customs tariffs.

12. C: Discontinued operations. A change in accounting principle occurs when an organization changes the method by which it records financial information. Examples of changes in accounting principles include switching from cash accounting to accrual accounting, changing a depreciation method or changing inventory methods from LIFO to FIFO. This change is recorded in the financial statements in the year in which the change occurred. The financial account in which this change is recorded is called the cumulative effect of a change in accounting principle and is part of the income statement. This change also requires an explanation in the notes to the financial statement, and the change must be justified.

13. B: Compounding interest. A rate of return is the gain or loss on an investment over a specific period of time. The rate of return measures an investment's earnings or losses against the initial investment amount purchased at a fixed point in time then producing cash flow at some point in the future. The cash flow may be in the form of dividends received while the investment is held, or capital gains realized when the investment is sold. Usually, the rate of return is adjusted so that the percentage is based on a one-year holding period. Compounding interest may play a part in determining the rate if the investment is held for longer than a year. The time value of money is also considered due to changing monetary rates in the international market. Inflation is also a factor in that it reduces the value of the money invested.

14. D: Investment risk. Standard deviation of return looks at an investment's annual rate of return to measure volatility and risk. It's also known as historical volatility. The higher the standard deviation, the more volatile a stock is considered. Expected gain is a measure of the most likely outcome of a gain or loss on an investment weighted by the chance of the gain or loss occurring. Coefficient of variation determines an investment's level of risk in relation to the financial markets.

15. B: Value at Risk. Value at Risk estimates how much an investment or a portfolio is likely to decrease over a short period of time under normal market conditions. It's measured using the amount of time the investment will be held, and a confidence level determined by historical price trends and volatility. Hedging is used to reduce risk caused by the price fluctuations of commodities. Diversification assumes that risk is reduced if a portfolio contains a diversity of investments; low-risk, low-return instruments along with investments that have a higher degree of risk and the capability of generating higher returns. Rate of return is the gain or loss incurred by an investment, and is a measure of profitability.

16. D: Cash dividends. Cash dividends, the most popular type of dividend, are paid when a corporation has earned income and excess cash on hand. Dividends are usually paid from accumulated earnings. Property dividends are a dividend paid in the form of inventory, land, equipment, or some other asset other than cash. A stock dividend is the issuance of additional shares of a corporation's stock to shareholders, proportional to number of shares owned so that percentage of ownership remains the same. Stock splits occur when old shares are replaced with a larger number of new shares. Stock splits reduce the market price per share of a corporation's stock by the ratio of the split. Other types of dividends include small stock dividends, large stock dividends, liquidating dividends and dividends on treasury stock.

17. B: Price/Book ratio. The Price/Book ratio is a stock's market price divided by its book value. The Price/Book ratio determines whether a stock is undervalued or overvalued. The Price/Earnings ratio is the ratio of the market price of a common stock divided by its earnings per share. It's used to compare the current earnings on common stock to predicted future earnings. The Price/Earnings ratio is an estimate of how much an investor is paying for a corporation's future earnings. A stock with a higher Price/Earnings ratio will be perceived to have a higher earnings potential. The Price/Sales ratio is the stock price divided by its per-share sales. This ratio determines whether the current market price of a stock is overpriced or underpriced.

18. A: Rate of return. Cost of capital is the rate of return a business needs to calculate to determine if making a capital investment, such as a new plant or machinery upgrade, is worthwhile. It includes the costs of debt and equity, and considers a rate of return a business might receive if it invested elsewhere. The ability of the organization to raise financing and how the financing will be made depends on this rate of return. Methods of financing may include issuing stock (equity financing) or borrowing (debt financing). For a project to be profitable, the rate of return must be greater than the cost of capital.

19. D: Owners retain same level of control. The major advantage of equity financing is that it's easier for small business to obtain capital without an obligation to repay the investment. However, equity financing would require the business' owners to relinquish a percentage of ownership and control in exchange for the funds. In addition, equity financing is more

difficult to administer than debt financing, and may require legal and accounting fees to do the necessary paperwork to comply with securities regulations. Often, providers of equity financing also provide advice and resources to help a business grow.

20. B: Concentration banking. Concentration banking is used to facilitate processing of customer payments when a company sells its product(s) in various states or countries. The business selects a bank in each geographic area to which customers in that area send their payments. Once funds are collected, each bank transfers the balance in the company's account to the company's main banking account. A lockbox is a box at a U. S. Post Office used to collect bill payments from customers, with those payments collected by the company's bank, then processed and deposited into the company's account. The bank also provides the company with a list of the customers who made payments and the amounts received from each customer. From this list, the company can update its accounts receivable records. . Electronic commerce (or e-commerce) is selling goods and services over the Internet.

21. D: Continuous review system. A continuous review system keeps a running total of inventory by logging each item as it enters and leaves inventory. When the inventory falls to a pre-determined level, the company will place more products into inventory to return to the base stock level. In the periodic review system, the inventory level is counted at specified periodic intervals. First-in, first-out is an inventory accounting method in which those products that have been in inventory the longest are the first products to be sold out of inventory. Conversely, last-in, first-out moves out items spending the shortest amount of time in inventory.

22. B: Securities Exchange Act of 1934. The Securities Exchange Act of 1934 was enacted to regulate the securities industry, the stock exchanges, securities broker-dealers, and others who worked in the industry. The Act made it mandatory for public companies to disclose financial and other information, and was the platform for launching the Securities and Exchange Commission (SEC). The Act requires companies to register their securities with the SEC prior to a public sale of the securities, and to disclose their financial information to the SEC and the investment community. The Sarbanes-Oxley Act of 2002 was put into law to protect investors from fraudulent accounting activities by publicly traded companies. Sarbanes-Oxley established the Public Company Accounting Oversight Board to oversee the audits of public companies in order to protect the interests of investors.

23. A: Unqualified opinion. An auditor issues an unqualified opinion report once he is confident a business' financial statements fairly represent its financial position. These statements must be prepared according to Generally Accepted Accounting Principles (GAAP), and the audit must comply with Generally Accepted Auditing Standards. The unqualified opinion with explanatory language report is used when a situation, such as a change in accounting principle, does not affect the unqualified opinion. The qualified opinion is given when there is a deviation from GAAP, but this deviation is not material. The adverse opinion is used when the deviation from GAAP is material and the organization will not change its financial statements. A disclaimer of opinion is given when the auditor feels that the deviation from GAAP is so severe that he cannot give an opinion as to the fairness of the financial statements.

24. B: Matrix organization. A matrix organization is structured based on performance and project needs by combining members from different departments to complete a project. A matrix organization may contain a mix of accounting, engineering, and sales personnel. A

functional organization structure is based on performance or job function, in which departments are created based on function, such as accounting, human resources, sales, and purchasing. A line organization structure is based on a singular function, with all jobs stemming from that function contained within the line structure. In a line-and-staff organization, the functions performed by the organization are outlined, and the departments that support these functions are associated with each function.

25. C: Banker's acceptance. A banker's acceptance is a short-term bill of exchange guaranteed by a bank. The bank guarantees that the issuer of the bill of exchange will pay the face value of the bill by the due date. If the issuer defaults on the bill, the bank pays the obligation. Letters of credit are used to guarantee that a buyer will pay for products received from a seller, and act as insurance for the buyer that the product will be received. Forfaiting is the purchase of the amount an importer owes an exporter. When these accounts receivable are purchased by the forfaiter, at a discount with cash, the importer is no longer obligated to pay the exporter, but the forfaiter. Countertrade is a nation's trading of their products for the products produced by another nation. Money is not used as a medium of exchange.

26. D: Markup percentage. Cost/volume/profit (CVP) analysis, also called break-even analysis, shows how costs and profits may change depending on the volume of output. It calculates the volume needed for total costs and total revenues to be equal. At this level, the company is considered to be "breaking even." CVP evaluates factors such as variable costs, fixed costs, sales price, production volume, and product mix to determine the possible amount of change in costs and profits. Once breakeven is established, management can determine the sales volume needed to earn a specific profit. CVP helps management understand how changes in the sales price and costs affect profits, and how a change in the product mix can affect the breakeven point and potential profits.

27. D: Utilities. Categories of expenses considered to be both fixed and variable include utilities and taxes. In these instances, a portion of the expenses need to be paid regardless of the level of production. For utilities, there is the fixed expense of a base fee that is not dependent on the amount of the resource used, and the remainder of the expense based on usage, which is variable. In addition, utilities will continue to be used during periods of no or low production activity. Variable costs are expenses, like materials and labor, which would vary depending on the level of production. Fixed costs, like rent, insurance, and salaries, would not ordinarily change with varying levels of production.

28. B: Material costs incurred by discontinuing a product. An avoidable cost is an expense that would not be incurred if a project or task is not undertaken. If a business discontinues a product, labor and material costs associated with that product are avoidable costs since the business will no longer incur them. An unavoidable cost is an expense incurred regardless of a decision to continue or suspend a project or task. If a product is discontinued, the business is still liable for rent and utilities. Unavoidable costs cannot be recovered or saved. Sunk costs, usually past expenditures, are costs paid as part of a project and cannot be changed by any action taken or decision made by a business. The purchase price would not be recovered by selling the item because the item is considered obsolete or has reached the end of its useful life. An opportunity cost is the cost of choosing one product over another. The cost is the benefit not received from the product that was not chosen. The opportunity cost of the product not chosen is income that would not be derived from the sale of that product.

29. C: The business cycle of the organization. Marginal analysis is an economic technique that measures incremental increases and decreases in an organization's operations. It measures the effects of changes when money, material, product, labor, or other factors fluctuate by one unit. It determines how these changes affect an organization's market, production, and business cycle. A make-or-buy decision compares the feasibility of producing a product in-house versus buying it from another supplier. It would be feasible to manufacture a product if the cost is lower, or if the business has excess capacity.

30. A: How the factors are measured. Qualitative factors are those in the decision making process that cannot be measured in monetary terms, whereas quantitative factors are measured in terms of money. Qualitative factors, such as employee morale and relationships with suppliers, have intrinsic value, and can enhance or detract from situations that do have value to the organization. Qualitative factors play an important role in the viability and long-term growth of an organization by augmenting its ability to run at a high level of production and help generate future profitability.

31. C: By need and buying behavior. Market segmentation is a method that first groups potential customers according to common needs, and then further groups them according to buying behavior. In this way, members of each individual segment can be predicted to respond similarly to a specific marketing technique. A segment can be based on demographic or psychographic information, such as where and how people live, age, geography, climate, or even political leaning.

32. D: The price of the product will decrease. A surplus occurs when too much of a product is available compared to the demand for that product. A surplus indicates that the price has been set too high. If the supply of a product is larger than the demand, the price of the product will decrease. This decrease in price will create a demand from people who were unwilling to buy at the higher price. A shortage occurs when there is not enough of a product on the market to satisfy the demand, indicating that the price is too low. Because of consumer competition for the product, the producers can raise their prices. This increase in price gives producers an incentive to produce more product to increase supply. This price increase can only continue until the amount being supplied meets the amount being demanded.

33. B: Discount and allowance pricing. Discount and allowance pricing offers incentives to customers to buy a product, these incentives may include coupons, cash rebates or seasonal discounts, and trade-in and promotional allowances. Segmented pricing varies the price points for a product depending on different segment characteristics. Psychological pricing uses motivational factors, such as the relationship between price and quality, to encourage a customer to purchase a product. Promotional pricing is when a product is temporarily reduced in price to help increase sales in the short-term. Geographical and international pricing may price products at different points depending on the demand in specific locations.

34. A: The percentage change in demand for one product divided by the percentage change in price to a second product. Cross elasticity of demand measures how the quantity demand of one good responds to price changes in another. It's calculated by dividing the percentage change in demand for a product by the percentage change in price of a second product. Price elasticity of supply measures how a change in price affects the quantity of a product

that producers are willing to supply, calculated by dividing the percentage change in supply by the percentage change in price. Price elasticity of demand measures consumer behavior, and shows the relationship between a quantity of demanded product and the increase or decrease in the price of that product. It's calculated by dividing the percent change in the quantity demanded by the percent change in price. Elasticity is the degree to which a demand or supply curve reacts to the price change of a product, calculated by dividing the percentage change in quantity by the percentage change in price.

35. D: The rate of return of the project. Capital budgeting is the process that tells a business whether a certain project or expenditure would be worth pursuing. Capital budgeting uses discounted cash flow methods, internal rates of return calculations, net present value methods, and payback periods to help make this decision. A value is assigned to the cash flow expected to be realized from the project or purchase of a real asset extending from time of acquisition through project completion or the life of the asset. Once cash flow is determined, it is discounted to its present value. Also considered in the capital budgeting process is the net investment for the organization; the cost of the project plus any installation costs less any proceeds from the disposal of the project. This process requires that a business look at the various costs and benefits involved in each of the investment alternatives being considered.

36. C: 10 years— for a company that dominates its market. Before forecasting cash flows for a capital project begins, a business must arrive at a forecast period; the duration of time in which the investment will generate cash flow in excess of its cost. A good rule of thumb is a 10-year forecast period for a business in a dominant market position, one year for a slow-growing organization, and five years for solid businesses with a proven sales record. Once the forecasting period is selected, a business can forecast revenue growth (future sales and profit margins). Although cash flows from the specific project are being forecast, they must be relevant in that they would affect a change to the business' existing overall cash flow.

37. C: Valuing mortgages and bonds. Internal rate of return is a discount rate that has a result of a net present value of zero. This discount rate is the expected return on the investment. It's used to decide if a long-term investment should be made. It's used most commonly for mortgages and bonds. Mortgages provide one cash inflow and a series of cash outflows, providing a consistent cash flow pattern and stable repayment schedule. Internal rate of return also works when comparing bonds with identical yields and terms. Net present value is used to evaluate which long-term project an organization should undertake. It evaluates the size and timing of future cash flows from a project and then discounts the cash flows to determine a dollar value for the cash flow in present dollars. Internal rate of return is easier to interpret than net present value.

38. A: Discounted cash flow analysis. Discounted cash flow analysis, used most often in business valuation, is a capital budgeting method that looks at the income and costs of an activity, project, or investment and evaluates each to determine a present value. It takes into consideration the flow of future cash income, the risk involved, and the timing of the cash flow. Because income is received over time, the further out the cash inflow, the higher the discount rate. The weighted average cost of capital is a method that helps a business decide whether or not to invest in a project by acquiring additional capital, either debt or equity. Weighted average cost of capital is used to measure the cost of capital for a project.

39. C: Investments with shorter payback periods have more liquidity and less risk. The payback period is the amount of time in which the cost of an investment is recovered, calculated by dividing initial investment cost by the annual cash inflows. The payback method assumes that annual cash inflows are equal from year to year. If they're not equal, a trial and error method needs to be assumed to determine an estimated payback period. When comparing two or more projects or investments, the better choice is the investment or project with the shortest payback period because of the assumption that shorter payback periods result in more liquidity and less risk.

40. A: Payback method. Payback method is not a true measure of profitability like net present value, internal rate of return, or discounted cash flow. The advantage of using the payback method is that it considers the risk involved in investing in a project. The disadvantages of using the payback method are that it does not take the time value of money into consideration, cash flows that occur after the payback period are not included in the calculation, and it does not factor in the scale or size of the investment.

41. D: Future cash flows received from the investment. Capital investment decisions are made based, in large part, on the expected rate of return The rate of return is dependent upon the amount, timing, risk, and time value of money. The amount, expressed as a percentage, is how much money the investment is expected to return. The timing is length of time that will elapse until the money will be repaid. The sooner the money is repaid, the higher the rate of return. The risk depends on how likely the money can be repaid at the expected rate within the expected time period, and if it can be repaid at all. The time value of money takes the present value of the future income into consideration. With riskier investments, the present value of the money returned in the future is less than the current value of the money.

42. B: Discounted cash flow and net present value. Deciding the scope and feasibility of a capital investment involves determining if positive net present value exists. The net present value calculation is applied using an appropriate discount rate. The project also needs to return a positive cash flow, one significant enough to provide a return to those who funded the project. Capital investment decisions are based on financing fixed assets and the capital structure of the financing. These decisions should only be pursued when the project maximizes the benefit to the business in the way of profits and value.

43. D: Decreases cash flow and increases risk. Capital investment financing affects a business' cash flow and contributes to the risk involved with the business' long-term viability. Capital investment financing could be a mix of debt and equity, with debt service being a liability that affects overall cash flow. Debt financing requires that the organization pay interest payment to service the debt. Equity financing does not produce the risk involved with debt financing, but it usually costs more and the business' owners will have a smaller ownership stake.

44. C: Standard deviation and coefficient of variation. Risk is measured using standard deviation and coefficient of variation statistics. Risk is the possibility that an investment will return an amount different than expected. It is a measure of the volatility of return on investment. The rule of risk is that a higher risk level would correspond to a higher return on investment, as compensation for the high risk. Risk analysis is a means to measure the amount of risk involved with investment decisions.

45. B: Sensitivity analysis. Sensitivity analysis is a method for dealing with wrong decisions, allowing the organization to review various decision alternatives using a "what-if" approach. It predicts the outcome of a wrong decision by looking at its effects on profits, costs, and sales. Sensitivity analysis also looks at what could happen if conditions related to a decision should change in the future, including ones both within and beyond the control of the organization. A certainty equivalent is the rate of return that an organization would need to realize in order for it to make a decision that has a higher level of risk and a higher, but uncertain, return on investment. Real options analysis is a method used in decision making to determine the best courses action to take with respect to future events.

46. D: Uncertainties are considered in the decision. A real option is a business' choice to pursue or not pursue a course of action with respect to an investment decision. Real options analysis, therefore, weighs these choices by evaluating potential outcomes arising from decisions. This approach gives a business the opportunity to think about what assets are at its disposal, an allows an organization to not only make a decision based on certainty, but to add uncertainties into the decision making process. Risk is the possibility that an investment will return an amount different than expected. It is a measure of the volatility of return on investment. Sensitivity analysis is a method for dealing with wrong decisions. A certainty equivalent is the rate of return that an organization would need to realize in order for it to make a decision that has a higher level of risk and a higher, but uncertain, return on investment. It measures this return against other risk-free investments.

47. B: To the appropriate authorities. A financial manager is expected to report illegal or fraudulent activity within an organization to the appropriate authorities. A financial manager must uphold several ethical behaviors and avoid conflicts of interest. Financial information must be prepared objectively and according to regulation, and presented fairly and accurately to shareholders, management and regulators, without shielding items that may be perceived as performance failures. A financial manager is also bound to uphold laws and regulations, and be objective, and must avoid both conflicts of economic interest and conflicts of professional interest.

48. C: Whistle blowing. The reasons for unethical behavior in the workplace are as varied as the individuals in that workplace. Organizational goals and standards may lead to unethical behavior. If managers and employees feel pressured to attain goals and standards, they may falsely submit records that do not accurately represent the work performed. The expectation of reaching a specified return on investment may lead to financial records being manipulated to show a higher return. Personality conflicts may lead to unethical behavior. When a subordinate lacks respect or confidence in a superior, that subordinate may take actions that undermine the superior's authority. In the decision making process, one or more individuals may unreasonably influence the group to vote in their favor and not in the best interest of the organization. Competition can also lead to unethical behavior. In order to generate sales, an individual or organization may revert to bribes or untruthful sales practices in order to obtain customers and revenues.

49. A: Proceeds from racketeering activities cannot be used to invest in a corporation. The Racketeer Influenced and Corrupt Organizations Act (RICO) was enacted in 1970 as a means of punishing organizations that participated in certain types of criminal activities. The original purpose of RICO was to eliminate the proliferation of organized crime in the U.S. These racketeering activities include gambling, bribery, extortion, bankruptcy fraud, mail fraud, securities fraud, prostitution, narcotics trafficking, loan sharking, and murder. Under

the provisions of RICO, proceeds from racketeering activities cannot be used to purchase an interest in an organization, and no individual associated with an organization may conduct racketeering activity through that organization. Individuals convicted of a RICO violation can be fined and sentenced to no more than 20 years in prison, and must forfeit any ownership in the organization in which the racketeering activity was transacted.

50. D: The Foreign Corrupt Practices Act of 1977. The Foreign Corrupt Practices Act of 1977 (FCPA) was enacted as a result of illegal acts of U.S. organizations committed in foreign countries. Most of these illegal acts were in the form of payments made to foreign governments and political parties as bribes to enter business relationships. These payments may appear in the financial records of an organization as overpayments, missing records, unrecorded transactions, misclassified costs, and re-transcription of records. The FCPA requires that all organizations falling under Securities and Exchange Commission (SEC) jurisdiction maintain internal accounting controls, and file regular reports to the SEC. The Business Ethics Advisory Council was created in response to the electrical equipment conspiracy cases in 1960. Recommendations made by this council caused large organizations to become aware of the problems associated with unethical behavior

Secret Key #1 - Time is Your Greatest Enemy

Pace Yourself

Wear a watch. At the beginning of the test, check the time (or start a chronometer on your watch to count the minutes), and check the time after every few questions to make sure you are "on schedule."

If you are forced to speed up, do it efficiently. Usually one or more answer choices can be eliminated without too much difficulty. Above all, don't panic. Don't speed up and just begin guessing at random choices. By pacing yourself, and continually monitoring your progress against your watch, you will always know exactly how far ahead or behind you are with your available time. If you find that you are one minute behind on the test, don't skip one question without spending any time on it, just to catch back up. Take 15 fewer seconds on the next four questions, and after four questions you'll have caught back up. Once you catch back up, you can continue working each problem at your normal pace.

Furthermore, don't dwell on the problems that you were rushed on. If a problem was taking up too much time and you made a hurried guess, it must be difficult. The difficult questions are the ones you are most likely to miss anyway, so it isn't a big loss. It is better to end with more time than you need than to run out of time.

Lastly, sometimes it is beneficial to slow down if you are constantly getting ahead of time. You are always more likely to catch a careless mistake by working more slowly than quickly, and among very high-scoring test takers (those who are likely to have lots of time left over), careless errors affect the score more than mastery of material.

Secret Key #2 - Guessing is not Guesswork

You probably know that guessing is a good idea. Unlike other standardized tests, there is no penalty for getting a wrong answer. Even if you have no idea about a question, you still have a 20-25% chance of getting it right.

Most test takers do not understand the impact that proper guessing can have on their score. Unless you score extremely high, guessing will significantly contribute to your final score.

Monkeys Take the Test

What most test takers don't realize is that to insure that 20-25% chance, you have to guess randomly. If you put 20 monkeys in a room to take this test, assuming they answered once per question and behaved themselves, on average they would get 20-25% of the questions correct. Put 20 test takers in the room, and the average will be much lower among guessed questions. Why?

    1. The test writers intentionally write deceptive answer choices that "look" right. A test

taker has no idea about a question, so he picks the "best looking" answer, which is often wrong. The monkey has no idea what looks good and what doesn't, so it will consistently be right about 20-25% of the time.

2. Test takers will eliminate answer choices from the guessing pool based on a hunch or intuition. Simple but correct answers often get excluded, leaving a 0% chance of being correct. The monkey has no clue, and often gets lucky with the best choice.

This is why the process of elimination endorsed by most test courses is flawed and detrimental to your performance. Test takers don't guess; they make an ignorant stab in the dark that is usually worse than random.

$5 Challenge

Let me introduce one of the most valuable ideas of this course—the $5 challenge:

You only mark your "best guess" if you are willing to bet $5 on it.
You only eliminate choices from guessing if you are willing to bet $5 on it.

Why $5? Five dollars is an amount of money that is small yet not insignificant, and can really add up fast (20 questions could cost you $100). Likewise, each answer choice on one question of the test will have a small impact on your overall score, but it can really add up to a lot of points in the end.

The process of elimination IS valuable. The following shows your chance of guessing it right:

If you eliminate wrong answer choices until only this many remain:	Chance of getting it correct:
1	100%
2	50%
3	33%

However, if you accidentally eliminate the right answer or go on a hunch for an incorrect answer, your chances drop dramatically—to 0%. By guessing among all the answer choices, you are GUARANTEED to have a shot at the right answer.

That's why the $5 test is so valuable. If you give up the advantage and safety of a pure guess, it had better be worth the risk.

What we still haven't covered is how to be sure that whatever guess you make is truly random. Here's the easiest way:

Always pick the first answer choice among those remaining.

Such a technique means that you have decided, **before you see a single test question**, exactly how you are going to guess, and since the order of choices tells you nothing about which one is correct, this guessing technique is perfectly random.

This section is not meant to scare you away from making educated guesses or eliminating choices; you just need to define when a choice is worth eliminating. The $5 test, along with a pre-defined random guessing strategy, is the best way to make sure you reap all of the benefits of guessing.

Secret Key #3 - Practice Smarter, Not Harder

Many test takers delay the test preparation process because they dread the awful amounts of practice time they think necessary to succeed on the test. We have refined an effective method that will take you only a fraction of the time.

There are a number of "obstacles" in the path to success. Among these are answering questions, finishing in time, and mastering test-taking strategies. All must be executed on the day of the test at peak performance, or your score will suffer. The test is a mental marathon that has a large impact on your future.

Just like a marathon runner, it is important to work your way up to the full challenge. So first you just worry about questions, and then time, and finally strategy:

Success Strategy

1. Find a good source for practice tests.
2. If you are willing to make a larger time investment, consider using more than one study guide. Often the different approaches of multiple authors will help you "get" difficult concepts.
3. Take a practice test with no time constraints, with all study helps, "open book." Take your time with questions and focus on applying strategies.
4. Take a practice test with time constraints, with all guides, "open book."
5. Take a final practice test without open material and with time limits.

If you have time to take more practice tests, just repeat step 5. By gradually exposing yourself to the full rigors of the test environment, you will condition your mind to the stress of test day and maximize your success.

Secret Key #4 - Prepare, Don't Procrastinate

Let me state an obvious fact: if you take the test three times, you will probably get three different scores. This is due to the way you feel on test day, the level of preparedness you have, and the version of the test you see. Despite the test writers' claims to the contrary, some versions of the test WILL be easier for you than others.

Since your future depends so much on your score, you should maximize your chances of success. In order to maximize the likelihood of success, you've got to prepare in advance.

This means taking practice tests and spending time learning the information and test taking strategies you will need to succeed.

Never go take the actual test as a "practice" test, expecting that you can just take it again if you need to. Take all the practice tests you can on your own, but when you go to take the official test, be prepared, be focused, and do your best the first time!

Secret Key #5 - Test Yourself

Everyone knows that time is money. There is no need to spend too much of your time or too little of your time preparing for the test. You should only spend as much of your precious time preparing as is necessary for you to get the score you need.

Once you have taken a practice test under real conditions of time constraints, then you will know if you are ready for the test or not.

If you have scored extremely high the first time that you take the practice test, then there is not much point in spending countless hours studying. You are already there.

Benchmark your abilities by retaking practice tests and seeing how much you have improved. Once you consistently score high enough to guarantee success, then you are ready.

If you have scored well below where you need, then knuckle down and begin studying in earnest. Check your improvement regularly through the use of practice tests under real conditions. Above all, don't worry, panic, or give up. The key is perseverance!

Then, when you go to take the test, remain confident and remember how well you did on the practice tests. If you can score high enough on a practice test, then you can do the same on the real thing.

General Strategies

The most important thing you can do is to ignore your fears and jump into the test immediately. Do not be overwhelmed by any strange-sounding terms. You have to jump into the test like jumping into a pool—all at once is the easiest way.

Make Predictions

As you read and understand the question, try to guess what the answer will be. Remember that several of the answer choices are wrong, and once you begin reading them, your mind will immediately become cluttered with answer choices designed to throw you off. Your mind is typically the most focused immediately after you have read the question and digested its contents. If you can, try to predict what the correct answer will be. You may be surprised at what you can predict.

Quickly scan the choices and see if your prediction is in the listed answer choices. If it is, then you can be quite confident that you have the right answer. It still won't hurt to check the other answer choices, but most of the time, you've got it!

Answer the Question

It may seem obvious to only pick answer choices that answer the question, but the test writers can create some excellent answer choices that are wrong. Don't pick an answer just because it sounds right, or you believe it to be true. It MUST answer the question. Once you've made your selection, always go back and check it against the question and make sure that you didn't misread the question and that the answer choice does answer the question posed.

Benchmark

After you read the first answer choice, decide if you think it sounds correct or not. If it doesn't, move on to the next answer choice. If it does, mentally mark that answer choice. This doesn't mean that you've definitely selected it as your answer choice, it just means that it's the best you've seen thus far. Go ahead and read the next choice. If the next choice is worse than the one you've already selected, keep going to the next answer choice. If the next choice is better than the choice you've already selected, mentally mark the new answer choice as your best guess.

The first answer choice that you select becomes your standard. Every other answer choice must be benchmarked against that standard. That choice is correct until proven otherwise by another answer choice beating it out. Once you've decided that no other answer choice seems as good, do one final check to ensure that your answer choice answers the question posed.

Valid Information

Don't discount any of the information provided in the question. Every piece of information may be necessary to determine the correct answer. None of the information in the question is there to throw you off (while the answer choices will certainly have information to throw you off). If two seemingly unrelated topics are discussed, don't ignore either. You can be confident there is a relationship, or it wouldn't be included in the question, and you are probably going to have to determine what is that relationship to find the answer.

Avoid "Fact Traps"

Don't get distracted by a choice that is factually true. Your search is for the answer that answers the question. Stay focused and don't fall for an answer that is true but irrelevant. Always go back to the question and make sure you're choosing an answer that actually answers the question and is not just a true statement. An answer can be factually correct, but it MUST answer the question asked. Additionally, two answers can both be seemingly correct, so be sure to read all of the answer choices, and make sure that you get the one that BEST answers the question.

Milk the Question

Some of the questions may throw you completely off. They might deal with a subject you have not been exposed to, or one that you haven't reviewed in years. While your lack of knowledge about the subject will be a hindrance, the question itself can give you many clues that will help you find the correct answer. Read the question carefully and look for clues. Watch particularly for adjectives and nouns describing difficult terms or words that you don't recognize. Regardless of whether you completely understand a word or not, replacing it with a synonym, either provided or one you more familiar with, may help you to understand what the questions are asking. Rather than wracking your mind about specific detailed information concerning a difficult term or word, try to use mental substitutes that are easier to understand.

The Trap of Familiarity

Don't just choose a word because you recognize it. On difficult questions, you may not recognize a number of words in the answer choices. The test writers don't put "make-believe" words on the test, so don't think that just because you only recognize all the words in one answer choice that that answer choice must be correct. If you only recognize words in one answer choice, then focus on that one. Is it correct? Try your best to determine if it is correct. If it is, that's great. If not, eliminate it. Each word and answer choice you eliminate increases your chances of getting the question correct, even if you then have to guess among the unfamiliar choices.

Eliminate Answers

Eliminate choices as soon as you realize they are wrong. But be careful! Make sure you consider all of the possible answer choices. Just because one appears right, doesn't mean that the next one won't be even better! The test writers will usually put more than one good answer choice for every question, so read all of them. Don't worry if you are stuck between two that seem right. By getting down to just two remaining possible choices, your odds are now 50/50. Rather than wasting too much time, play the odds. You are guessing, but guessing wisely because you've been able to knock out some of the answer choices that you know are wrong. If you are eliminating choices and realize that the last answer choice you are left with is also obviously wrong, don't panic. Start over and consider each choice again. There may easily be something that you missed the first time and will realize on the second pass.

Tough Questions

If you are stumped on a problem or it appears too hard or too difficult, don't waste time. Move on! Remember though, if you can quickly check for obviously incorrect answer choices, your chances of guessing correctly are greatly improved. Before you completely give up, at least try to knock out a couple of possible answers. Eliminate what you can and then guess at the remaining answer choices before moving on.

Brainstorm

If you get stuck on a difficult question, spend a few seconds quickly brainstorming. Run through the complete list of possible answer choices. Look at each choice and ask yourself, "Could this answer the question satisfactorily?" Go through each answer choice and consider it independently of the others. By systematically going through all possibilities, you may find something that you would otherwise overlook. Remember though that when you get stuck, it's important to try to keep moving.

Read Carefully

Understand the problem. Read the question and answer choices carefully. Don't miss the question because you misread the terms. You have plenty of time to read each question thoroughly and make sure you understand what is being asked. Yet a happy medium must be attained, so don't waste too much time. You must read carefully, but efficiently.

Face Value

When in doubt, use common sense. Always accept the situation in the problem at face value. Don't read too much into it. These problems will not require you to make huge leaps of logic. The test writers aren't trying to throw you off with a cheap trick. If you have to go beyond creativity and make a leap of logic in order to have an answer choice answer the question, then you should look at the other answer choices. Don't overcomplicate the problem by creating theoretical relationships or explanations that will warp time or space. These are normal problems rooted in reality. It's just that the applicable relationship or explanation may not be readily apparent and you have to figure things out. Use your common sense to interpret anything that isn't clear.

Prefixes

If you're having trouble with a word in the question or answer choices, try dissecting it. Take advantage of every clue that the word might include. Prefixes and suffixes can be a huge help. Usually they allow you to determine a basic meaning. Pre- means before, post- means after, pro - is positive, de- is negative. From these prefixes and suffixes, you can get an idea of the general meaning of the word and try to put it into context. Beware though of any traps. Just because con- is the opposite of pro-, doesn't necessarily mean congress is the opposite of progress!

Hedge Phrases

Watch out for critical hedge phrases, led off with words such as "likely," "may," "can," "sometimes," "often," "almost," "mostly," "usually," "generally," "rarely," and "sometimes." Question writers insert these hedge phrases to cover every possibility. Often an answer choice will be wrong simply because it leaves no room for exception. Unless the situation calls for them, avoid answer choices that have definitive words like "exactly," and "always."

Switchback Words

Stay alert for "switchbacks." These are the words and phrases frequently used to alert you to shifts in thought. The most common switchback word is "but." Others include "although," "however," "nevertheless," "on the other hand," "even though," "while," "in spite of," "despite," and "regardless of."

New Information

Correct answer choices will rarely have completely new information included. Answer choices typically are straightforward reflections of the material asked about and will directly relate to the question. If a new piece of information is included in an answer choice that doesn't even seem to relate to the topic being asked about, then that answer choice is likely incorrect. All of the information needed to answer the question is usually provided for you in the question. You should not have to make guesses that are unsupported or choose answer choices that require unknown information that cannot be reasoned from what is given.

Time Management

On technical questions, don't get lost on the technical terms. Don't spend too much time on any one question. If you don't know what a term means, then odds are you aren't going to get much further since you don't have a dictionary. You should be able to immediately recognize whether or not you know a term. If you don't, work with the other clues that you have—the other answer choices and terms provided—but don't waste too much time trying to figure out a difficult term that you don't know.

Contextual Clues

Look for contextual clues. An answer can be right but not the correct answer. The contextual clues will help you find the answer that is most right and is correct. Understand the context in which a phrase or statement is made. This will help you make important distinctions.

Don't Panic

Panicking will not answer any questions for you; therefore, it isn't helpful. When you first see the question, if your mind goes blank, take a deep breath. Force yourself to mechanically go through the steps of solving the problem using the strategies you've learned.

Pace Yourself

Don't get clock fever. It's easy to be overwhelmed when you're looking at a page full of questions, your mind is full of random thoughts and feeling confused, and the clock is ticking down faster than you would like. Calm down and maintain the pace that you have set for yourself. As long as you are on track by monitoring your pace, you are guaranteed to have enough time for yourself. When you get to the last few minutes of the test, it may seem like you won't have enough time left, but if you only have as many questions as you should have left at that point, then you're right on track!

Answer Selection

The best way to pick an answer choice is to eliminate all of those that are wrong, until only one is left and confirm that is the correct answer. Sometimes though, an answer choice may immediately look right. Be careful! Take a second to make sure that the other choices are not equally obvious. Don't make a hasty mistake. There are only two times that you should stop before checking other answers. First is when you are positive that the answer choice you have selected is correct. Second is when time is almost out and you have to make a quick guess!

Check Your Work

Since you will probably not know every term listed and the answer to every question, it is important that you get credit for the ones that you do know. Don't miss any questions through careless mistakes. If at all possible, try to take a second to look back over your answer selection and make sure you've selected the correct answer choice and haven't made a costly careless mistake (such as marking an answer choice that you didn't mean to mark). The time it takes for this quick double check should more than pay for itself in caught mistakes.

Beware of Directly Quoted Answers

Sometimes an answer choice will repeat word for word a portion of the question or reference section. However, beware of such exact duplication. It may be a trap! More than likely, the correct choice will paraphrase or summarize a point, rather than being exactly the same wording.

Slang

Scientific sounding answers are better than slang ones. An answer choice that begins "To compare the outcomes..." is much more likely to be correct than one that begins "Because some people insisted..."

Extreme Statements

Avoid wild answers that throw out highly controversial ideas that are proclaimed as established fact. An answer choice that states the "process should used in certain situations, if..." is much more likely to be correct than one that states the "process should be discontinued completely." The first is a calm rational statement and doesn't even make a definitive, uncompromising stance, using a hedge word "if" to provide wiggle room, whereas the second choice is a radical idea and far more extreme.

Answer Choice Families

When you have two or more answer choices that are direct opposites or parallels, one of them is usually the correct answer. For instance, if one answer choice states "x increases" and another answer choice states "x decreases" or "y increases," then those two or three answer choices are very similar in construction and fall into the same family of answer choices. A family of answer choices consists of two or three answer choices, very similar in construction, but often with directly opposite meanings. Usually the correct answer choice will be in that family of answer choices. The "odd man out" or answer choice that doesn't seem to fit the parallel construction of the other answer choices is more likely to be incorrect.

Special Report: How to Overcome Test Anxiety

The very nature of tests caters to some level of anxiety, nervousness, or tension, just as we feel for any important event that occurs in our lives. A little bit of anxiety or nervousness can be a good thing. It helps us with motivation, and makes achievement just that much sweeter. However, too much anxiety can be a problem, especially if it hinders our ability to function and perform.

"Test anxiety," is the term that refers to the emotional reactions that some test-takers experience when faced with a test or exam. Having a fear of testing and exams is based upon a rational fear, since the test-taker's performance can shape the course of an academic career. Nevertheless, experiencing excessive fear of examinations will only interfere with the test-taker's ability to perform and chance to be successful.

There are a large variety of causes that can contribute to the development and sensation of test anxiety. These include, but are not limited to, lack of preparation and worrying about issues surrounding the test.

Lack of Preparation

Lack of preparation can be identified by the following behaviors or situations:

Not scheduling enough time to study, and therefore cramming the night before the test or exam
Managing time poorly, to create the sensation that there is not enough time to do everything
Failing to organize the text information in advance, so that the study material consists of the entire text and not simply the pertinent information
Poor overall studying habits

Worrying, on the other hand, can be related to both the test taker, or many other factors around him/her that will be affected by the results of the test. These include worrying about:

Previous performances on similar exams, or exams in general
How friends and other students are achieving
The negative consequences that will result from a poor grade or failure

There are three primary elements to test anxiety. Physical components, which involve the same typical bodily reactions as those to acute anxiety (to be discussed below). Emotional factors have to do with fear or panic. Mental or cognitive issues concerning attention spans and memory abilities.

Physical Signals

There are many different symptoms of test anxiety, and these are not limited to mental and emotional strain. Frequently there are a range of physical signals that will let a test taker know that he/she is suffering from test anxiety. These bodily changes can include the following:

Perspiring
Sweaty palms
Wet, trembling hands
Nausea
Dry mouth
A knot in the stomach
Headache
Faintness
Muscle tension
Aching shoulders, back and neck
Rapid heart beat
Feeling too hot/cold

To recognize the sensation of test anxiety, a test-taker should monitor him/herself for the following sensations:

The physical distress symptoms as listed above
Emotional sensitivity, expressing emotional feelings such as the need to cry or laugh too much, or a sensation of anger or helplessness
A decreased ability to think, causing the test-taker to blank out or have racing thoughts that are hard to organize or control.

Though most students will feel some level of anxiety when faced with a test or exam, the majority can cope with that anxiety and maintain it at a manageable level. However, those who cannot are faced with a very real and very serious condition, which can and should be controlled for the immeasurable benefit of this sufferer.

Naturally, these sensations lead to negative results for the testing experience. The most common effects of test anxiety have to do with nervousness and mental blocking.

Nervousness

Nervousness can appear in several different levels:

The test-taker's difficulty, or even inability to read and understand the questions on the test
The difficulty or inability to organize thoughts to a coherent form
The difficulty or inability to recall key words and concepts relating to the testing questions (especially essays)
The receipt of poor grades on a test, though the test material was well known by the test taker

Conversely, a person may also experience mental blocking, which involves:

Blanking out on test questions
Only remembering the correct answers to the questions when the test has already finished.

Fortunately for test anxiety sufferers, beating these feelings, to a large degree, has to do with proper preparation. When a test taker has a feeling of preparedness, then anxiety will be dramatically lessened.

The first step to resolving anxiety issues is to distinguish which of the two types of anxiety are being suffered. If the anxiety is a direct result of a lack of preparation, this should be considered a normal reaction, and the anxiety level (as opposed to the test results) shouldn't be anything to worry about. However, if, when adequately prepared, the test-taker still panics, blanks out, or seems to overreact, this is not a fully rational reaction. While this can be considered normal too, there are many ways to combat and overcome these effects.

Remember that anxiety cannot be entirely eliminated, however, there are ways to minimize it, to make the anxiety easier to manage. Preparation is one of the best ways to minimize test anxiety. Therefore the following techniques are wise in order to best fight off any anxiety that may want to build.

To begin with, try to avoid cramming before a test, whenever it is possible. By trying to memorize an entire term's worth of information in one day, you'll be shocking your system, and not giving yourself a very good chance to absorb the information. This is an easy path to anxiety, so for those who suffer from test anxiety, cramming should not even be considered an option.

Instead of cramming, work throughout the semester to combine all of the material which is presented throughout the semester, and work on it gradually as the course goes by, making sure to master the main concepts first, leaving minor details for a week or so before the test.

To study for the upcoming exam, be sure to pose questions that may be on the examination, to gauge the ability to answer them by integrating the ideas from your texts, notes and lectures, as well as any supplementary readings.

If it is truly impossible to cover all of the information that was covered in that particular term, concentrate on the most important portions, that can be covered very well. Learn these concepts as best as possible, so that when the test comes, a goal can be made to use these concepts as presentations of your knowledge.

In addition to study habits, changes in attitude are critical to beating a struggle with test anxiety. In fact, an improvement of the perspective over the entire test-taking experience can actually help a test taker to enjoy studying and therefore improve the overall experience. Be certain not to overemphasize the significance of the grade - know that the result of the test is neither a reflection of self worth, nor is it a measure of intelligence; one grade will not predict a person's future success.

To improve an overall testing outlook, the following steps should be tried:

Keeping in mind that the most reasonable expectation for taking a test is to expect to try to demonstrate as much of what you know as you possibly can.
Reminding ourselves that a test is only one test; this is not the only one, and there will be others.
The thought of thinking of oneself in an irrational, all-or-nothing term should be avoided at all costs.
A reward should be designated for after the test, so there's something to look forward to. Whether it be going to a movie, going out to eat, or simply visiting friends, schedule it in advance, and do it no matter what result is expected on the exam.

Test-takers should also keep in mind that the basics are some of the most important things, even beyond anti-anxiety techniques and studying. Never neglect the basic social, emotional and biological needs, in order to try to absorb information. In order to best achieve, these three factors must be held as just as important as the studying itself.

Study Steps

Remember the following important steps for studying:

Maintain healthy nutrition and exercise habits. Continue both your recreational activities and social pass times. These both contribute to your physical and emotional well being.
Be certain to get a good amount of sleep, especially the night before the test, because when you're overtired you are not able to perform to the best of your best ability.
Keep the studying pace to a moderate level by taking breaks when they are needed, and varying the work whenever possible, to keep the mind fresh instead of getting bored.
When enough studying has been done that all the material that can be learned has been learned, and the test taker is prepared for the test, stop studying and do something relaxing such as listening to music, watching a movie, or taking a warm bubble bath.

There are also many other techniques to minimize the uneasiness or apprehension that is experienced along with test anxiety before, during, or even after the examination. In fact, there are a great deal of things that can be done to stop anxiety from interfering with lifestyle and performance. Again, remember that anxiety will not be eliminated entirely, and it shouldn't be. Otherwise that "up" feeling for exams would not exist, and most of us depend on that sensation to perform better than usual. However, this anxiety has to be at a level that is manageable.

Of course, as we have just discussed, being prepared for the exam is half the battle right away. Attending all classes, finding out what knowledge will be expected on the exam, and knowing the exam schedules are easy steps to lowering anxiety. Keeping up with work will remove the need to cram, and efficient study habits will eliminate wasted time. Studying should be done in an ideal location for concentration, so that it is simple to become interested in the material and give it complete attention. A method such as SQ3R (Survey, Question, Read, Recite, Review) is a wonderful key to follow to make sure that the study habits are as effective as possible, especially in the case of learning from a textbook. Flashcards are great techniques for memorization. Learning to take good notes will mean that notes will be full of useful information, so that less sifting will need to be done to seek out what is pertinent for studying. Reviewing notes after class and then again on occasion will keep the information fresh in the mind. From notes that have been taken summary sheets and outlines can be made for simpler reviewing.

A study group can also be a very motivational and helpful place to study, as there will be a sharing of ideas, all of the minds can work together, to make sure that everyone understands, and the studying will be made more interesting because it will be a social occasion.

Basically, though, as long as the test-taker remains organized and self confident, with efficient study habits, less time will need to be spent studying, and higher grades will be achieved.

To become self confident, there are many useful steps. The first of these is "self talk." It has been shown through extensive research, that self-talk for students who suffer from test anxiety, should be well monitored, in order to make sure that it contributes to self confidence as opposed to sinking the student. Frequently the self talk of test-anxious students is negative or self-defeating, thinking that everyone else is smarter and faster, that they always mess up, and that if they don't do well, they'll fail the entire course. It is important to decreasing anxiety that awareness is made of self talk. Try writing any negative self thoughts and then disputing them with a positive statement instead. Begin self-encouragement as though it was a friend speaking. Repeat positive statements to help reprogram the mind to believing in successes instead of failures.

Helpful Techniques

Other extremely helpful techniques include:

Self-visualization of doing well and reaching goals
While aiming for an "A" level of understanding, don't try to "overprotect" by setting your expectations lower. This will only convince the mind to stop studying in order to meet the lower expectations.
Don't make comparisons with the results or habits of other students. These are individual factors, and different things work for different people, causing different results.
Strive to become an expert in learning what works well, and what can be done in order to improve. Consider collecting this data in a journal.
Create rewards for after studying instead of doing things before studying that will only turn into avoidance behaviors.
Make a practice of relaxing - by using methods such as progressive relaxation, self-hypnosis, guided imagery, etc - in order to make relaxation an automatic sensation.
Work on creating a state of relaxed concentration so that concentrating will take on the focus of the mind, so that none will be wasted on worrying.
Take good care of the physical self by eating well and getting enough sleep.
Plan in time for exercise and stick to this plan.

Beyond these techniques, there are other methods to be used before, during and after the test that will help the test-taker perform well in addition to overcoming anxiety.

Before the exam comes the academic preparation. This involves establishing a study schedule and beginning at least one week before the actual date of the test. By doing this, the anxiety of not having enough time to study for the test will be automatically eliminated. Moreover, this will make the studying a much more effective experience, ensuring that the learning will be an easier process. This relieves much undue pressure on the test-taker.

Summary sheets, note cards, and flash cards with the main concepts and examples of these main concepts should be prepared in advance of the actual studying time. A topic should never be eliminated from this process. By omitting a topic because it isn't expected to be on the test is only setting up the test-taker for anxiety should it actually appear on the exam. Utilize the course syllabus for laying out the topics that should be studied. Carefully go over the notes that were made in class, paying special attention to any of the issues that the professor took special care to emphasize while lecturing in class. In the textbooks, use the chapter review, or if possible, the chapter tests, to begin your review.

It may even be possible to ask the instructor what information will be covered on the exam, or what the format of the exam will be (for example, multiple choice, essay, free form, true-false). Additionally, see if it is possible to find out how many questions will be on the test. If a review sheet or sample test has been offered by the professor, make good use of it, above anything else, for the preparation for the test. Another great resource for getting to know the examination is reviewing tests from previous semesters. Use these tests to review, and aim to achieve a 100% score on each of the possible topics. With a few exceptions, the goal that you set for yourself is the highest one that you will reach.

Take all of the questions that were assigned as homework, and rework them to any other possible course material. The more problems reworked, the more skill and confidence will form as a result. When forming the solution to a problem, write out each of the steps. Don't simply do head work. By doing as many steps on paper as possible, much clarification and therefore confidence will be formed. Do this with as many homework problems as possible, before checking the answers. By checking the answer after each problem, a reinforcement will exist, that will not be on the exam. Study situations should be as exam-like as possible, to prime the test-taker's system for the experience. By waiting to check the answers at the end, a psychological advantage will be formed, to decrease the stress factor.

Another fantastic reason for not cramming is the avoidance of confusion in concepts, especially when it comes to mathematics. 8-10 hours of study will become one hundred percent more effective if it is spread out over a week or at least several days, instead of doing it all in one sitting. Recognize that the human brain requires time in order to assimilate new material, so frequent breaks and a span of study time over several days will be much more beneficial.

Additionally, don't study right up until the point of the exam. Studying should stop a minimum of one hour before the exam begins. This allows the brain to rest and put things in their proper order. This will also provide the time to become as relaxed as possible when going into the examination room. The test-taker will also have time to eat well and eat sensibly. Know that the brain needs food as much as the rest of the body. With enough food and enough sleep, as well as a relaxed attitude, the body and the mind are primed for success.

Avoid any anxious classmates who are talking about the exam. These students only spread anxiety, and are not worth sharing the anxious sentimentalities.

Before the test also involves creating a positive attitude, so mental preparation should also be a point of concentration. There are many keys to creating a positive attitude. Should fears become rushing in, make a visualization of taking the exam, doing well, and seeing an A written on the paper. Write out a list of affirmations that will bring a feeling of confidence, such as "I am doing well in my English class," "I studied well and know my material," "I enjoy this class." Even if the affirmations aren't believed at first, it sends a positive message to the subconscious which will result in an alteration of the overall belief system, which is the system that creates reality.

If a sensation of panic begins, work with the fear and imagine the very worst! Work through the entire scenario of not passing the test, failing the entire course, and dropping out of school, followed by not getting a job, and pushing a shopping cart through the dark alley where you'll live. This will place things into perspective! Then, practice deep breathing and create a visualization of the opposite situation - achieving an "A" on the exam, passing the entire course, receiving the degree at a graduation ceremony.

On the day of the test, there are many things to be done to ensure the best results, as well as the most calm outlook. The following stages are suggested in order to maximize test-taking potential:

Begin the examination day with a moderate breakfast, and avoid any coffee or beverages with caffeine if the test taker is prone to jitters. Even people who are used to managing caffeine can feel jittery or light-headed when it is taken on a test day. Attempt to do something that is relaxing before the examination begins. As last minute cramming clouds the mastering of overall concepts, it is better to use this time to create a calming outlook.
Be certain to arrive at the test location well in advance, in order to provide time to select a location that is away from doors, windows and other distractions, as well as giving enough time to relax before the test begins.
Keep away from anxiety generating classmates who will upset the sensation of stability and relaxation that is being attempted before the exam.
Should the waiting period before the exam begins cause anxiety, create a self-distraction by reading a light magazine or something else that is relaxing and simple.

During the exam itself, read the entire exam from beginning to end, and find out how much time should be allotted to each individual problem. Once writing the exam, should more time be taken for a problem, it should be abandoned, in order to begin another problem. If there is time at the end, the unfinished problem can always be returned to and completed.

Read the instructions very carefully - twice - so that unpleasant surprises won't follow during or after the exam has ended.

When writing the exam, pretend that the situation is actually simply the completion of homework within a library, or at home. This will assist in forming a relaxed atmosphere, and will allow the brain extra focus for the complex thinking function.

Begin the exam with all of the questions with which the most confidence is felt. This will build the confidence level regarding the entire exam and will begin a quality momentum. This will also create encouragement for trying the problems where uncertainty resides.

Going with the "gut instinct" is always the way to go when solving a problem. Second guessing should be avoided at all costs. Have confidence in the ability to do well.

For essay questions, create an outline in advance that will keep the mind organized and make certain that all of the points are remembered. For multiple choice, read every answer, even if the correct one has been spotted - a better one may exist.

Continue at a pace that is reasonable and not rushed, in order to be able to work carefully. Provide enough time to go over the answers at the end, to check for small errors that can be corrected.

Should a feeling of panic begin, breathe deeply, and think of the feeling of the body releasing sand through its pores. Visualize a calm, peaceful place, and include all of the sights, sounds and sensations of this image. Continue the deep breathing, and take a few minutes to continue this with closed eyes. When all is well again, return to the test.

If a "blanking" occurs for a certain question, skip it and move on to the next question. There will be time to return to the other question later. Get everything done that can be done, first, to guarantee all the grades that can be compiled, and to build all of the confidence possible. Then return to the weaker questions to build the marks from there.

Remember, one's own reality can be created, so as long as the belief is there, success will follow. And remember: anxiety can happen later, right now, there's an exam to be written!

After the examination is complete, whether there is a feeling for a good grade or a bad grade, don't dwell on the exam, and be certain to follow through on the reward that was promised...and enjoy it! Don't dwell on any mistakes that have been made, as there is nothing that can be done at this point anyway.

Additionally, don't begin to study for the next test right away. Do something relaxing for a while, and let the mind relax and prepare itself to begin absorbing information again.

From the results of the exam - both the grade and the entire experience, be certain to learn from what has gone on. Perfect studying habits and work some more on confidence in order to make the next examination experience even better than the last one.

Learn to avoid places where openings occurred for laziness, procrastination and day dreaming.

Use the time between this exam and the next one to better learn to relax, even learning to relax on cue, so that any anxiety can be controlled during the next exam. Learn how to relax the body. Slouch in your chair if that helps. Tighten and then relax all of the different muscle groups, one group at a time, beginning with the feet and then working all the way up to the neck and face. This will ultimately relax the muscles more than they were to begin with. Learn how to breathe deeply and comfortably, and focus on this breathing going in and out as a relaxing thought. With every exhale, repeat the word "relax."

As common as test anxiety is, it is very possible to overcome it. Make yourself one of the test-takers who overcome this frustrating hindrance.

Additional Bonus Material

Due to our efforts to try to keep this book to a manageable length, we've created a link that will give you access to all of your additional bonus material.

Please visit http://www.mometrix.com/bonus948/cmap2fdm to access the information.